For Competitive Exams

Vedic
Mathematics

MADE EASY

For Competitive Exams

Vedic Mathematics

MADE EASY

**Learn the Ancient Wisdom of Fast Track
Calculations in Simplified Ways !**

Pandit Ramnandan Shashtri

Arihant Publications (I) Pvt. Ltd, Meerut

ॐ **Administrative & Production Offices**

Corporate Office: 4577/15, Agarwal Road, Darya Ganj, New Delhi -110002
Tele: 011- 4730600, 23280316; Fax: 011- 23280316
Head Office: Kalindi, TP Nagar, Meerut (UP) - 250002
Tele: 0121-2401479, 2512970, 4004199; Fax: 0121-2401648

All disputes subject to Meerut (UP) jurisdiction only.

ॐ **Sales & Support Offices**

Agra, Bengaluru, Bhubaneswar, Delhi(I&II), Guwahati, Haldwani, Hyderabad, Jaipur, Kolkata, Kota, Lucknow, Nagpur, Meerut & Patna

ॐ **ISBN :** 978-81-8348-624-8

ॐ **Price:** ₹ 110
Typeset by Mittal DTP Unit at Meerut

For further information about the products from Arihant,
log on to www.arihantbooks.com or email to info@arihantbooks.com

preface

'Vedic Mathematics' is the ancient system of mathematics; a unique technique of calculations based on simple rules and principles, with which any mathematical problem - be it arithmetic, algebra, geometry or trigonometry–can be solved, ORALLY !! According to Clive Middleton, a vedic maths enthusiast, "These formulas describe the way the mind naturally works, and are therefore a great help in directing the student to the appropriate method of solution."

In today's system of competitive examinations where speed with accuracy is the calling shot, a mastery & practice of vedic maths can work wonder for the aspirants. Not only the students or the aspirants of various competitive exams, even the professionals, like, engineers, teachers, executives, or businessmen can benefit immensely from Vedic Mathematics.

Divided into 21 chapters, this book is the outcome of a thorough research on Vedic Maths, its 'Sutras' and their best possible applications, which has been scientifically synchronized with the learning pace & pattern of different categories of readers. Each of the chapters is followed by two exercises, one with questions on the topics taught in the chapter along with their hints & solutions; and the other exercise comprises questions from various competitive and management entrances, the solutions for which has been given at the end of the chapters, together. Approach and language of the book is simple & lucid, and the format of presenting texts is attractive enough to keep the mind of the readers engrossed.

The book bears all the hallmarks of brand Arihant & its years of experience as leading publisher in competitive examination segment.

We invite and welcome any feedback/suggestion for improvement of this book in subsequent editions.

Varanasi, 2011   **Pt. Ramnandan Shastri**

contents

‖ Vedic mathematics ‖
what is it ?

Born in the Vedic Age, but buried under centuries of debris, this remarkable system of calculation was deciphered towards the beginning of the 20th century, when there was a great interest in ancient Sanskrit texts, especially in Europe. However, certain texts called Ganita Sutras, which contained mathematical deductions, were ignored, because no one could find any mathematics in them. These texts, it's believed, bore the germs of what we now know as Vedic Mathematics.

What is Vedic Mathematics?

'Vedic Mathematics' is the name given to the ancient system of mathematics, or, to be precise, a unique technique of calculations based on simple rules and principles, with which any mathematical problem - be it arithmetic, algebra, geometry or trigonometry - can be solved, ORALLY !!

Some may wonder why it is called "vedic" . Just as the basic principles of Hinduism lie in the Vedas, so do the roots of mathematics. The Vedas, written around 1500-900 BCE, are ancient Indian texts containing a record of human experience and knowledge. Thousands of years ago, Vedic mathematicians authored various theses and dissertations on mathematics. It is now commonly believed and widely accepted that these treatises laid down the foundations of algebra, algorithm, square roots, cube roots, various methods of calculation, and the concept of zero.

The system is based on 16 Vedic sutras or aphorisms, which are actually word-formulae describing natural ways of solving a whole range of mathematical problems. Some examples of Sutras are "By one more than the one before", "All from 9 & the last from 10", and "Vertically & Crosswise". These 16 one-line formulae originally written in Sanskrit, which can be easily memorized, enables one to solve long mathematical problems quickly.

Bharati Krishna Tirtha ji & Vedic Math

Bharati Krishna Tirtha ji

The revival of Vedic Mathematics is no less than a miracle. Extracting the theorems and corollaries from religious texts requires not only an understanding of the scriptures but also a genuinely intelligent mind.

Credit of rediscovering Vedic maths (between 1911 and 1918) from the ancient Indian scriptures goes to Sri Bharati Krishna Tirthaji (1884-1960), a scholar of Sanskrit, Mathematics, History and Philosophy. He studied these ancient texts for years, and after careful investigation was able to reconstruct a series of mathematical formulae called Sutras.

Bharati Krishna Tirthaji, who was also the former Shankaracharya (major religious leader) of Puri, India, delved into the ancient Vedic texts and established the techniques of this system in his pioneering work - Vedic Mathematics (1965), which is considered the starting point for all work on Vedic math. It is said that after Bharati Krishna's original 16 volumes of work expounding the Vedic system were lost, in his final years he wrote this single volume, which was published five years after his death.

Development of Vedic Math

Vedic math was immediately hailed as a new alternative system of mathematics, when a copy of the book reached London in the late 1960s. Some British mathematicians, including Kenneth Williams, Andrew Nicholas and Jeremy Pickles took interest in this new system. They extended the introductory material of Bharati Krishna's book, and delivered lectures on it in London. In 1981, this was collated into a book entitled Introductory Lectures on Vedic Mathematics. A few successive trips to India by Andrew Nicholas between 1981 and 1987, renewed the interest on Vedic math, and scholars and teachers in India started taking it seriously.

The Sutras (aphorisms) apply to and cover each and every part of each and every chapter of each and every branch of mathematics (including arithmetic, algebra, geometry – plane and solid, trigonometry – plane and spherical, conics- geometrical and analytical, astronomy, calculus – differential and integral etc., etc. In fact, there is no part of mathematics, pure or applied, which is beyond their jurisdiction;

The Sutras are easy to understand, easy to apply and easy to remember; and the whole work can be truthfully summarised in one word "mental"!

Dr L M Singhvi, the former High Commissioner of India in the UK, also an avid endorser of the system says: "A single sutra would generally encompass a varied and wide range of particular applications and may be likened to a programmed chip of our computer age".

Another Vedic maths enthusiast, Clive Middleton feels, "These formulae describe the way the mind naturally works, and are therefore a great help in directing the student to the appropriate method of solution."

The Sub Sutras

Together with the sixteen Sutras ,Sri Bharati Krishna Tirthaji lists thirteen sub-Sutras. For example Proportionately, By Alternate Elimination and Retention and By Mere Observation are three of them. Two of the sixteen Sutras (By One More than the One Before and By Addition and By Subtraction) are indicated to be sub-Sutras also. However it is believed that although there are exactly sixteen Sutras, the sub-Sutras are not fixed in number.

The Growing Interest in Vedic Math

Quite a few years ago, a few schools in Europe started teaching Vedic Maths on experimental basis. Today this remarkable system is taught in many schools and institutes in India and abroad, and even to MBA and economics students. Interest in Vedic maths is growing in the field of education where mathematics students are looking for a new and better approach to the subject. Even students at the Indian Institute of Technology (IIT) are said to be using this ancient technique for quick calculations. No wonder, in a Convocation speech addressed to the students of IIT, Delhi, by Dr. Murli Manohar Joshi, former Union Minister for Science & Technology, stressed the significance of Vedic maths, while pointing out the important contributions of India in the realm of Mathematics, such as Aryabhatta, who laid the foundations of algebra, Baudhayan, the great geometer, and Medhatithi and Madhyatithi, the saint duo, who formulated the basic framework for numerals

Researches are being undertaken in many areas, including the effects of learning Vedic maths on children. A great deal of research is also being done on how to develop more powerful and easy applications of the Vedic sutras in geometry, calculus, and computing.

Vedic Maths
(Some FAQs)

Q. Can Vedic Maths be used to facilitate the students of higher classes to remember complicated Maths formulae?

A. Yes. Concepts such as Quadratic Equations, Simultaneous Equations, Trigonometry, Even Calculus has been made simple and easier in Vedic Mathematics.

Q. How does knowledge in Vedic Math help a student to minimize careless mistakes?

A. In Vedic Mathematics, the mental one-line formulae are such that it has an inbuilt system of series of checks. The student can't go wrong. Failure is not an option in Vedic Mathematics. Hence Vedic Mathematics helps to boost the confidence of the student as success leads to success and this brings out the true potential of the student.

Q. To whom Vedic Maths is beneficial?

A. Students, Competitive exam aspirants, Engineers, Professionals, Teachers, Executives, Parents and even Businessmen can benefit from Vedic Mathematics.

Vedic Maths is helpful to software developers as it helps them to do their coding and programming as it is more scientific than the normal system of mathematics

Q. Some critics feel that 'arithmetic as is speeded up by application of the sutras can be performed on a computer or calculator anyway, making their knowledge rather irrelevant in the modern world'.

A. According to a study conducted some years ago by a university in the United States, the constant use of calculators for more than twenty years by person atrophies his brain significantly. We have all met shopkeepers who use calculators to determine what 10+5 is. Don't you find it silly?

Our Brain is a muscle. Just like the body needs exercise the brain needs it too. Through Vedic mathematics you use both the parts of your brain- the left and the right hence keeping you mentally agile even in your old age when the brain functions less.

Moreover I would like to add that some calculators are even prone to errors. Try this on your calculator 2+3 x 4 and get an answer. If your calculator shows 20 and not 14 your answer is incorrect. J Any Guesses Why?

How Vedic Maths could be useful to students preparing for competitive exams?

Vedic Mathematics is emerging as a useful tool for students appearing in competitive examinations like SAT, iSAT, CAT,MAT,XAT, GRE, Engineering Entrance examinations.... where speed and accuracy plays a crucial role.

A system of mental calculation based on the Atharvaveda, an ancient Vedic text, Vedic mathematics can speed up arithmetic calculation and has applications to more advanced mathematics, such as calculus and linear algebra. Calculations are carried out mentally — students can invent their own methods, there is no one 'correct' method.

Can you find out how many matches are played during the Wimbledon tennis championship, based on the information that the first round has 64 games, the next 32 until you reach the quarter-finals, semi-finals and the final?

The conventional approach is to add the number of games: 64+ 32+16+8+4+2+1 to get to the answer, 127. Try the Vedic approach: Since there are 128 players (2 x 64) and only one person wins the competition, there must be 127 losers and for each loser there is a match, so there are 127 matches.

Vedic Mathematics simplifies the four basic mathematical operations like addition, subtraction, multiplication and division. This will reduce the time to solve a mathematical problem, especially in examination halls.

For example, if we have to multiply 86 and 98, the conventional method is

$$\begin{array}{r} 86 \\ \times 98 \\ \hline 688 \\ 774 \\ \hline 8428 \end{array}$$

But by the method of Vedic Mathematics we can do it in a simple way. The two numbers are set down (Here numbers are 86 and 98) and their difference from a suitable base are written (Here we can take the base 100) down to the right (that is 100-86 = 14 and 100-98 = 02).

athematics we can do it in a simple way. The two numbers are set down (Here numbers are 86 and 98) and their difference from a suitable base are written (Here we can take the base 100) down to the right (that is 100-86 = 14 and 100-98 = 02).

$$\begin{array}{r} 86 - 14 \\ 98 - 02 \\ \hline 84/28 \end{array}$$

Ans: 8428

The answer comes out in two parts. The sign"/" is used here to separate these two parts. To get the first part, cross subtract, either 86-2=84 or 98-14 To get the second part multiply the difference of the number from the base chosen. ie 14×2=28. Now 28 is the second part of the answer. Hence the answer is 8428.

It is a useful tool in finding squeres and cubes of number. In Vedic Mathematics there is a fantastic method to square numbers ending in 5. Competitive examinations. In the final analysis we can see that the real losers in the competitive examination are persons without any systematic time management. On the other hand the performers overcome "Time factor" through the systematic tackling of time traps". To hear the news of victory, to conqurer tomorrow, to keep the presence in the current and upcoming cutthroat competitions, we can find a good companion in Vedic Mathematics.

In a talk in 1958 at the Institute of Technology, Pasadena, California, USA Sri Bharati Krishna Tirthaji said: "People who have practical knowledge of the application of the sutras, need not go in for the theory side of it at all". This fascinating comment makes a clear distinction between those who learn to do mathematics by just practising the Sutras and those who can also learn the theory of it as well. The non-mathematician and the applied mathematician just want to use mathematics. There are those of us who just want to get on and do the job and those who want to understand the details.

Anyone familiar with Vedic system will know that it is more integrated, more efficient and more fun than conventional mathematics. It leads to greater flexibility of mind, increased mental agility and stimulates the creative faculty that is in all students. However, further research is needed to establish the nature of the Sutras and their full range of application.

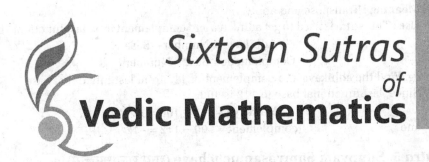

Sixteen Sutras of Vedic Mathematics

Sutra 1. Ekādhikena Pūrvena (एकाधिकेन पूर्वेण)

Meaning : By one more than the one before.

Use : This sutra is used to get a next number to given number.

eg, To get a next number to 96,

add 1 to 96, thus next number = 96 + 1 = 97.

Sutra 2. Nikhilam Navatas'caramam Dasatah (निखिलं नवतश्चरमं दशतः)

Meaning : All from nine and the last from ten.

Use : This sutra is used to get a complement number from its functional base.

eg, To get a complement number of 1369 (from functional base 10000).

Subtract 1, 3 , 6 from 9 and last digit 9 from 10.

$$9 - 1 = 8, \quad 9 - 3 = 6, \quad 9 - 6 = 3, \quad 10 - 9 = 1$$

Thus, required number = 8631

If a number has zero in the end, take first non-zero number as last and then write zeroes in the end.

eg, To get a complement number of 4700. Take 47, subtract 4 from 9 and 7 from 10.

Thus, $\qquad 9 - 4 = 5$

and $\qquad 10 - 7 = 3.$

Hence, $\qquad 53$

⇒ *So,* 5300 *is complement to* 4700.

Sutra 3. Ūrdhva-tiryagbhyam (ऊर्ध्वतिर्यग्भ्याम्)

Meaning : Vertically and crosswise

Use : This sutra is used to multiply numbers vertically and crosswise.

eg, Vertical and crosswise multiplication of (8, 9, 5) and (1, 2, 3).

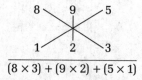

$$(8 \times 3) + (9 \times 2) + (5 \times 1)$$

Sutra 4. Parāvartya Yojayet (परावर्त्य योजयेत्)

Meaning : Transpose and apply.

Use : This sutra is used to get adhikaya and complement from last functional base.

$$\text{Adhikaya} = \text{Number} - \text{Base}$$
$$\text{Complement} = \text{Base} - \text{Number}$$

eg, Find the adhikaya and complement of 112 from last functional base.

Since, last functional base to 112 is 100.

∴ $$\text{Adhikaya} = 112 - 100 = 12$$

and $$\text{complement} = 100 - 112 = -12$$

Sutra 5. Shunyam Sāmyasamuchchaye (शून्यं साम्यसमुच्चये)

Meaning : If the samuchchaya is the same, it is zero.

Use : This sutra is used to determine a such number which is common to all, that must be equal to zero. This may use in the following ways.

(i) If in any equation any term is common, that term is equal to zero.

eg, $7 (x + 6) + 2 (x + 6) (x - 2) + (x + 6)(x - 1) = 0$

Here, $(x + 6)$ is common to all terms. Thus,

$$x + 6 = 0$$

(ii) If the product of independent terms in an equation are same, then variable is equal to zero.

eg, $$(y + 3)(y + 6) = (y + 2)(y + 9)$$

∵ $$3 \times 6 = 2 \times 9$$

∴ $$y = 0$$

(iii) If the numerators of two fractions are same, the sum of both denominators is equal to zero.

eg, In $\dfrac{7}{6x + 1} + \dfrac{7}{2x - 1} = 0$, numerators of both fractions are same, then the

sum of denominators is equal to zero.

∴ $$6x + 1 + 2x - 1 = 0$$

⇒ $$x = 0$$

(iv) If the sum of Nr and Dr of fractions in an equation are equal, then that sum is equal to zero.

eg, In $\dfrac{6x + 3}{5x + 2} = \dfrac{5x + 2}{6x + 3}$

Sum of Nr $= 6x + 3 + 5x + 2 =$ Sum of Dr

∴ $$(6x + 3) + (5x + 2) = 0$$

(v) If two expressions are equal, then on subtracting one from another, the resultant is zero.

eg, $(a+b)^3$ and $a^3 + b^3 + 3ab(a+b)$ are same.

∴ $(a+b)^3 - (a^3 + b^3 + 3ab(a+b)) = 0$

Sutra 6. Āanyarūpaye Sūnyamanyat (आन्यरूपये शून्यंअन्यत्)

Meaning : If one is the ratio, the other is zero.

Use : This sutra is used to find the value of one variable, if in a system of linear equations, the ratio of coefficients of other variable is equal to the ratio of constant terms.

The value of required variable is zero.

eg,
$$12x + 78y = 24$$
$$16x + 76y = 32$$

Here, ratio of coefficients of x is equal to ratio of constant terms.

ie, $12:16::24:32$

Thus, the value of other variable y is zero.

Sutra 7. Sankalana Vyavakalanābhyam (संकलनव्यकलनाभ्याम्)

Meaning : By addition and subtraction.

Use : This sutra is used to find the value of variables in a system of linear equations, if the coefficients of variables are found interchanged.

eg, The given system of simultaneous linear equations is

$$45x - 23y = 113 \qquad \text{...(i)}$$

and $$23x - 45y = 91 \qquad \text{...(ii)}$$

The coefficients are found interchanged. Thus, the value of variables can be obtained by adding and subtracting these equations.

On adding Eqs. (i) and (ii), we get

$$x - y = 3 \qquad \text{...(iii)}$$

On subtracting Eq. (ii) from Eq. (i), we get

$$x + y = 1 \qquad \text{...(iv)}$$

On solving Eqs. (iii) and (iv), we get

$$x = 2 \quad \text{and} \quad y = -1$$

Sutra 8. Purna Puranabhyam (पूरण पूरणभ्यां)

Meaning : By the completion or non-completion.

Use : This sutra is used to find the value of variable by making equation perfect square or perfect cube.

eg, (i) Find the value of $(x - y)$, if $x + y = 10$ and $xy = 9$.

Now, make $(x - y)$ a perfect square.

ie, $(x - y)^2 = (x + y)^2 - 4xy$

$= 10^2 - 4 \times 9 = 100 - 36 = 64$

⇒ $x - y = \pm 8$

(ii) Find the value of x in $x^3 + 6x^2 + 11x + 6 = 0$

Since, $x^3 + 6x^2 + 12x + 8 = (x + 2)^3$

$$\therefore \qquad x^3 + 6x^2 + 11x + 6 + x + 2 = x + 2$$
$$\Rightarrow \qquad x^3 + 6x^2 + 12x + 8 = x + 2$$
$$\Rightarrow \qquad (x+2)^3 = (x+2)$$
$$\Rightarrow \qquad (x+2)^3 - (x+2) = 0$$
$$\Rightarrow \qquad x + 2 = 0, (x+2)^2 = 1$$
$$\Rightarrow \qquad x = -2, x + 2 = \pm 1$$
$$\Rightarrow \qquad x = -2, -1, -3.$$

Sutra 9. Chalana-kalanabhyam (चलनकलनाभ्याम्)

Meaning : Differential calculus.

Use : This sutra is used in following two cases.

(i) To find the roots of a quadratic.

(ii) To factorizing expressions of 3rd, 4th and 5th degree.

The proper use of this sutra will be clearly explained in the chapter "Factorisation and Differential Calculus".

Sutra 10. Yavadunam (यावदूनम्)

Meaning : By the deficiency.

Use : This sutra is used in following two cases.

(i) To find the complement to the nearest functional base.

eg, The nearest functional base to 112 is 100, then its complement

$$= 100 - 112 = -12 = \overline{12}$$

(ii) Also, used to find the direct cube of two digits numbers.

ie, if the number is xy, then

$$x^3 \quad x^2 y \quad xy^2 \quad y^3$$
$$2x^2 y \quad 2xy^2$$

Sum them up taking care of carryovers.

eg, To find the cube of 12.

1	2	4	8
	4	8	
1	7	2	8

$$\therefore \qquad 12^3 = 1728.$$

Sutra 11. Vyasti Samastih (व्यष्टि समष्टिः)

Meaning : Specific and general.

Use : This sutra is used in the following two cases

(i) To find the average

$$\text{Average} = \frac{\text{Sum of data}}{\text{Total number of data}}$$

eg, Find the average of 13, 14, 15.

$$\text{Average} = \frac{13 + 14 + 15}{3} = \frac{42}{3} = 14$$

(ii) HCF = Product of common factors
Find the HCF of 24 and 36.

$$\begin{array}{r|l} 2 & 24,\ 36 \\ \hline 2 & 12,\ 18 \\ \hline 3 & 6,\ 9 \\ \hline & 2,\ 3 \end{array}$$

$\therefore$ HCF = Product of common factors =

$= 2 \times 2 \times 3 = 12$

and   LCM = (Product of common factors) × (Product of specific multiples)

Sutra 12. Sesanyankena Caramena (शेषायङ्क्रेन चरमेण)

Meaning : The remainders by the last digit.
Use : This sutra is used to express a fraction as a decimal, to all its decimal places. This sutra will be much clearly explained in further chapters.

Sutra 13. Sopantyadvayamantyam (सोपान्त्यद्वयमन्तयम्)

Meaning : The ultimate and twice the penultimate.
Use : This sutra is used to find the value of variable which is such that in equation $\dfrac{1}{AB} + \dfrac{1}{AC} = \dfrac{1}{AD} + \dfrac{1}{BC}$ and A, B, C, D are in AP, then $D + 2C = 0$ is one solution.

eg,   In $\dfrac{1}{x^2 + 5x + 6} + \dfrac{1}{x^2 + 6x + 8} = \dfrac{1}{x^2 + 7x + 10} + \dfrac{1}{x^2 + 7x + 12}$

$\Rightarrow \dfrac{1}{(x+2)(x+3)} + \dfrac{1}{(x+2)(x+4)} = \dfrac{1}{(x+2)(x+5)} + \dfrac{1}{(x+3)(x+4)}$

$A = x + 2, B = x + 3, C = x + 4$ and $D = x + 5$

Also, A, B, C and D are AP.

$\therefore \qquad x + 5 + 2(x + 4) = 0 \qquad \Rightarrow \ x + 5 + 2x + 8 = 0$

$\Rightarrow \qquad\qquad 3x = -13 \quad \Rightarrow \quad x = \dfrac{-13}{3}$

Sutra 14. Ekanyunena Purvena (एकन्यूनेन पूर्वेण)

Meaning : By one less than the one before.
Use : This sutra is used in following three cases
   (i) To find a number one less than the given number.
      eg, The number one less than to 9879 is $9879 - 1 = 9878$.
   (ii) To multiply the two numbers in which a number is in repeating 9's.
      eg, 878×9999
      Step I $\qquad\qquad 0878 - 1 = 877$
      Step II $\qquad\qquad 9999 - 877 = 9122$
      $\therefore \qquad\qquad 878 \times 9999 = 8779122.$
   (iii) In expressing a fraction into decimal.

Sutra 15. Gunitasamuchchaya (गुणितसमुच्चयः)

Meaning : The product of the sum.
Use : This sutra is used to verify the factors of an expression with its a corallary.

If we factorise a quadratic or cubic, the sum of coefficients of an equation is equal to the product of sum of coefficients of factors.

eg, $$x^2 + 5x + 6 = (x + 3)(x + 2)$$

$\therefore$ Sum of coefficients in $x^2 + 5x + 6 = 1 + 5 + 6 = 12$

and product of sum of coefficients of factors = $(1 + 3) \times (1 + 2) = 4 \times 3 = 12$.

Sutra 16. Gunakasamuchchaya (गुणकसमुच्चय)

Meaning : All the multipliers.

Use : This sutra is used in the following three cases

(i) To find the number of zeroes in the product.

eg, Find the number of zeroes in the product of 400 and 4000.

$\therefore$ Number of zeroes in the product = $2 + 3 = 5$

(ii) To find the place of decimal in the product of numbers.

eg, Find the place of decimal in the product 1.02 and 2.3734.

Since, decimal in 1.02 is after second place and decimal in 2.3734 is after fourth place.

$\therefore$ The decimal in the product is after $2 + 4 = 6$th place

(iii) $a^m \times a^n = a^{m+n}$ eg, $a^5 \times a^5 = a^{5+5} = a^{10}$

Sixteen Upasūtras of Vedic Mathematics

S.No.	Sutra	Explanation
1.	आनुरूप्येण (Anurupyena)	Proportionately
2.	शिष्यते शेषसंज्ञः (Sisyate Sesasmjnah)	The remainder remains constant
3.	आद्यमाद्ये नान्त्यमन्त्येन (Adyamadye Nantyamantyena)	The first by the first and the last by the last
4.	केवलैः सप्तकं गुण्यात् (Kevalaih Saptakam Gunyat)	For seven, the multiplier is 143
5.	वेष्टनम् (Vestanam)	By osculation
6.	यावइनं तावदूनम् (Yavadunam Tavadunam)	Less on by the deficiency
7.	यावइनं तावदूनीकृत्य वर्गंच योजयेत् (Yavadunam Tavadunikritya Vargancha Yojayet)	Whatever the deficiency, less on by that amount and set up the square of the deficiency
8.	अन्त्ययोर्दशकेऽपि (Antyayordashake 'pi')	Last totalling ten
9.	अन्त्ययोरेव (Antyayoreva)	Only the last terms
10.	समुच्चय गुणितः (Samuchchaya Gunitah)	The sum of the products
11.	लोपनस्थापनाभ्याम् (Lopanasthapanabhayam)	By alternate elimination and retention
12.	विलोकनम् (Vilokanam)	Mere observation
13.	गुणित समुच्यकः समुच्चय गुणितः (Gunita Samuchchaya Samuchchaya Gunitah)	The product of the sum is the sum of the products
14.	ध्वजाङ्क (Dhvajanka)	On the flag
15.	द्वन्द्वयोग (Dwandwa Yoga)	Duplex combination process
16.	शुद्धः (Sudha)	Purification

Addition

Addition

In mathematics, there are four fundamental operation in which addition is most frequently used to combine different values.

In addition, one has to remember carry forward values at several places but inadvertently ignored which gives a wrong result.

To overcome this difficulty, we use a vedic mathematical sutra **"Ekadhiken Poorvena"** (एकाधिकेन पूर्वेण) which means **"by one more than the one before"**.

In this system, there is no need to remember the carry forward values. Since, in this method whenever in the process of addition the value greater than nine is obtained, carry forward value is marked by the point (·) above the left side digit and on the stage at which point digits are added, we add one in the resultant number.

Example 1 *Add* 1234 *and* 1972.

Solution

$$
\begin{array}{r}
\overset{\cdot}{1}\ \overset{\cdot}{2}\ 3\ 4 \\
+\ 1\ 9\ 7\ 2 \\
\hline
3\ 2\ 0\ 6 \\
\end{array}
\qquad
\begin{cases}
4 + 2 = 6 \\
3 + 7 = 10 \\
9 + 2 + \underline{1} = 12 \\
\qquad\qquad \text{Value of point} \\
1 + 1 + \underline{1} = 3
\end{cases}
$$

Example 2 *Add* 17329, 36097 *and* 68379.

Solution

$$
\begin{array}{r}
\overset{\cdot}{1}\ 7\ \overset{\cdot}{3}\ \overset{\cdot}{2}\ 9 \\
\overset{\cdot}{3}\ 6\ \overset{\cdot}{0}\ 9\ 7 \\
+\ 6\ 8\ 3\ 7\ 9 \\
\hline
12\ 1\ 8\ 0\ 5 \\
\end{array}
\qquad
\begin{cases}
9 + 7 + 9 = 25 \\
2 + 9 + 7 + \underline{1} + \underline{1} = 20 \\
3 + 3 + \underline{1} + \underline{1} = 8 \\
7 + 6 + 8 = 21 \\
6 + 3 + 1 + \underline{1} + \underline{1} = 12
\end{cases}
$$

Underlined "1" is value of a point.

Addition Using Zero Ending Numbers

The numbers which are ended with zero, are called zero ending numbers. *eg*, 10, 20, 50, 400, etc are zero ending numbers.

In oral addition, we use this method.

In this method, we take a zero ending number nearest to one of given number. We add the another number by subtracting the difference of zero ending number and first given number from another number. This will be much clear in the following examples.

Example 3 *Add* 187 *and* 23 *by using zero ending numbers.*

Solution Since, 190 is nearest zero ending number to 187.

Now, we add $23 - (190 - 187)$ ie, $23 - 3$ ie, 20 in 190.

$$\therefore \qquad 187 + 23 = 190 + 20$$
$$= 210$$

Example 4 *Add* 299 *and* 31 *using zero ending numbers.*

Solution Since, 300 is nearest zero ending number to 299.

Now, we add $31 - (300 - 299)$ ie, $31 - 1$ ie, 30 in 300.

$$\therefore \qquad 299 + 31 = 300 + 30$$
$$= 330$$

Verification of Answer

To verify the answer, the sum of digits of given numbers must be equal to the sum of digits of resultant number.

In this process, we should know that sum of digits must be a digit not a number. If it is a number, then find the sum of its digits.

It will be much clear in the following example.

Example 5 *Add* 9378 *and* 2895. *Also, verify your answer.*

Solution

$$
\begin{array}{r}
9378 \\
\bullet\bullet\bullet \\
+\ 2895 \\
\hline
12273 \\
\hline
\end{array}
\qquad
\begin{cases}
8 + 5 = 13 \\
9 + 7 + \underline{1} = 17 \\
8 + 3 + \underline{1} = 12 \\
9 + 2 + \underline{1} = 12
\end{cases}
$$

Now, sum of digits of given numbers

$$= 9 + 3 + 7 + 8 + 2 + 8 + 9 + 5$$
$$= 51 = 5 + 1 = 6$$

and sum of digits of resultant number

$$= 1 + 2 + 2 + 7 + 3$$
$$= 15 = 1 + 5 = 6$$

$\because$ Sum of digits of given numbers is equal to the sum of digits of resultant number. Hence, our answer is correct.

*Sum of digits of number is called **Bijank** of that number.*

Addition of Algebraic Expressions

This method of addition is helpful in single variable polynomial. First thing to understand, the representation of coefficient of polynomials.

ie,

Polynomials		Coefficients of variable				
$7x + 2$					7	2
$3x^2 + 5x + 1$				3	5	1
$x^3 + x + 1$ *ie,*			1	0	1	1
$x^3 + 0x^2 + x + 1$						
$x^4 - 7x^3 + 3x - 5$	1	$\bar{7}$	0	3	$\bar{5}$	

Please noted that the terms containing negative sign, that sign must be kept in the form of bar over a coefficient.

Now, we add the coefficients in vertical position. We also kept it in mind that a coefficient having bar, that must be subtracted, *ie,*

$$
\begin{array}{ccccc}
& 7 & 2 & & \\
& 3 & 5 & 1 & \\
1 & 0 & 1 & 1 & \\
\hline
1\bar{7} & 0 & 3 & \bar{5} & \\
\hline
1\,\bar{6}\, & 3 & (16)\, & \bar{1} &
\end{array}
\qquad
\begin{cases}
2 + 1 + 1 - 5 = -1 \\
7 + 5 + 1 + 3 = (16) \\
3 + 0 + 0 = 3 \\
1 - 7 = -6
\end{cases}
$$

∴ Resultant polynomial is $x^4 - 6x^3 + 3x^2 + 16x - 1$.

Example 6   *Add* $3x^3 + 5x^2 + 9$, $4x^4 + 2x + 3$ *and* $2x^2 + x + 8$.

Solution

Polynomials		Coefficients of variable			
$3x^3 + 5x^2 + 9$			3	5	0	9
$4x^4 + 2x + 3$ *ie,* $4x^4 + 0x^3 + 0x^2 + 2x + 3$	4	0	0	2	3
$2x^2 + x + 8$				2	1	8
	4	3	7	3	(20)

∴ Resultant polynomial is $4x^4 + 3x^3 + 7x^2 + 3x + 20$.

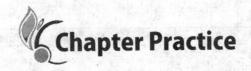

Chapter Practice

Exercise 1

1. Add using "Ekadhikena Poorvena."
   - (i) 237 and 34
   - (ii) 187 and 384
   - (iii) 763 and 169
   - (iv) 889 and 894
   - (v) 459 and 235
   - (vi) 999 and 282
   - (vii) 347 and 487
   - (viii) 787 and 375
   - (ix) 847 and 328
   - (x) 184 and 114
   - (xi) 3478, 6854 and 8470
   - (xii) 3075, 1780 and 3289
   - (xiii) 46437 and 35578
   - (xiv) 543789 and 268289
   - (xv) 19568 and 9265
   - (xvi) 90523471 and 73567819
   - (xvii) 696, 65301, 26829 and 543757
   - (xviii) 46379, 37584 and 19686
   - (xix) 1178, 119, 11257 and 12916
   - (xx) 9052, 3471, 5678 and 3125

2. Add using zero ending numbers. Also, verify your answer.
   - (i) 27 and 34
   - (ii) 187 and 35
   - (iii) 63 and 88
   - (iv) 38 and 27
   - (v) 187 and 23
   - (vi) 299 and 43
   - (vii) 479 and 224
   - (viii) 218 and 7
   - (ix) 9999 and 124
   - (x) 99982 and 88

3. Add the following polynomials using vedic method.
   - (i) $x + 3$ and $3x^2 + 5$
   - (ii) $x^3 + x + 1$ and $x^2 + x - 1$
   - (iii) $x^5 - 6x^2, x^4 + x^3 + 6x^2 + 8x + 2$ and $x^2 - 7x + 9$
   - (iv) $x^4 - 3x^3 + 8x^2 + 7x + 9$ and $x^3 + 6x^2 + 2x + 7$
   - (v) $6x^5 + 4x^4 + 7x^3 + 8x^2 + 3x + 6, x^6 - 1$ and $x^3 + 6x^2 + 2x + 7$

Exercise 2

1. $3596 + 2123 + 5472$ is equal to   **(Bank Clerk, 09)**
   - (a) 11911
   - (b) 19111
   - (c) 11119
   - (d) 11191

2. If $58321 + 69386 = x + 37098$, x is equal to   **(Bank Clerk, 09)**
   - (a) 91619
   - (b) 90609
   - (c) 92609
   - (d) 8961

3. $1834 + 2458$ is equal to   **(Bank Clerk, 09)**
   - (a) 4298
   - (b) 4292
   - (c) 4922
   - (d) None of these

4. $15368 + 8153$ is equal to   **(Bank Clerk, 09)**
   - (a) 23521
   - (b) 25321
   - (c) 23251
   - (d) None of these

5. 3412 + 4367 + 5590 is equal to   (Bank Clerk, 09)

   (a) 13121   (b) 13245

   (c) 13369   (d) 13487

6. 5555 + 555 + 55 is equal to   (Bank Clerk, 09)

   (a) 6555   (b) 6165

   (c) 6665   (d) 55555

7. 7414 + 3698 + 1257 + 1869 is equal to   (SBI, 09)

   (a) 14238   (b) 74438

   (c) 13428   (d) 73248

8. 8484 + 4248 + 2112 + 1074 + 513 is equal to

   (a) 16441   (b) 16341

   (c) 16431   (d) 1631

9. The sum of $x^3 + x + 1$ and $6x^2 + 5$ is

   (a) $x^3 - 5x - 4$ (b) $x^3 + 7x + 6$

   (c) $x^3 + 6x^2 + x + 6$ (d) None of these

10. The sum of $x + 3$ and $x^3 + 9x^2 + 11x + 7$ is

   (a) $x^3 + 9x^2 + 12x + 10$ (b) $x^3 + 10x^2 + 11x + 10$

   (c) $x^3 + 9x^2 + 2x + 10$ (d) None of these

Answers

Exercise 1

1.   (i) 271   (ii) 571   (iii) 932   (iv) 1783

     (v) 694   (vi) 1281   (vii) 834   (viii) 1162

    (ix) 1175   (x) 298   (xi) 18802   (xii) 8144

  (xiii) 82015   (xiv) 812078   (xv) 28833   (xvi) 164091290

  (xvii) 636583   (xviii) 103649   (xix) 25470   (xx) 21326

2.   (i) 61   (ii) 222   (iii) 151   (iv) 65

     (v) 210   (vi) 342   (vii) 703   (viii) 225

    (ix) 10123   (x) 100070

3.   (i) $3x^2 + x + 8$

    (ii) $x^3 + x^2 + 2x$

   (iii) $x^5 + x^4 + x^3 + x^2 + x + 11$

   (iv) $x^4 - 2x^3 + 14x^2 + 9x + 16$

    (v) $x^6 + 6x^5 + 4x^4 + 8x^3 + 14x^2 + 5x + 12$

Exercise 2

1. (d)	2. (b)	3. (b)	4. (a)	5. (c)
6. (b)	7. (a)	8. (c)	9. (c)	10. (a)

2 Subtraction

Subtraction is a fundamental operation in Mathematics, which is often used to find the difference between two given numbers. Sometimes it also termed as inverse of addition. In the process of subtraction using vedic method, sutras "Ekadhikena Poorvena", "Ekanyunena Poorvena" or " Nikhilum Navataha Charmam Dashtaha" can be used for numbers and for polynomials we can use vedic sutra "Paravartya Yojayet." which means "Transpose and Apply."

Subtraction Using "Ekadhikena Poorvena"

For numbers using vedic sutra "Ekadhikena Poorvena", we follow the following process.

To subtract a number (subtrahand) from another number, subtract the digits from right, if the digit of subtrahand is greater, then put a dot (•) on the next to the left and subtract that digit from (10+number). Now, to subtract a dotted digit, that should be increased by one and this process continued upto to an end.

This method will be much clear in the following examples.

Example 1 *Subtract* 16889 *from* 36875.

Solution
$$
\begin{array}{r}
3\ 6\ 8\ 7\ 5 \\
\bullet\ \bullet\ \bullet \\
1\ 6\ 8\ 8\ 9 \\
\hline
1\ 9\ 9\ 8\ 6
\end{array}
$$

It is not possible to subtract 9 from 5. Put a dot (•) next to the left (*ie*, 8) of a subtrahand and subtract 9 from 15 *ie*, $15-9=6$.

Now, to subtract a dotted 8, subtract $8+1$ *ie*, 9 from 7, which is not possible, so as above process put a dot (•) on next 8 and subtract 9 from 17 *ie*, $17-9=8$.

Similarly,
$$18-9=9$$
$$16-7=9$$
and
$$3-2=1$$

Thus, $36875 - 16889 = 19986$

Example 2 *Subtract* 19568 *from* 30125.

Solution
$$
\begin{array}{r}
3\ 0\ 1\ 2\ 5 \\
\bullet\ \bullet\ \bullet\ \bullet \\
1\ 9\ 5\ 6\ 8 \\
\hline
1\ 0\ 5\ 5\ 7
\end{array}
$$

To subtract 8 from 5, put a dot (•) on next to the number 6 and subtract 8 from 15.

ie, $\qquad$ $15 - 8 = 7$

Now, to subtract 6 from 2, put a dot on 5 and subtract 7 from 12.

ie, $\qquad$ $12 - 7 = 5$

Similarly, $\qquad$ $11 - 6 = 5$

$\qquad$ $10 - 10 = 0$

and $\qquad$ $3 - 2 = 1$

Thus, $\qquad$ $30125 - 19568 = 10557$

❦Subtraction Using "Ekanyunena Poorvena"

For numbers we use vedic sutra "Ekanyunena Poorvena." We follow the following process.

For getting the difference, the value is borrowed, the dot (•) is put below the left side digit of upper value (minuend) and when the difference is taken at that stage first point mark value is reduced.

This process will be much clear in the following examples.

Example 3 *Subtract* 6788 *from* 7397.

Solution $\qquad$
```
7 3 9 7
  •   •
6 7 8 8
0 6 0 9
```

To subtract 8 from 7, put a dot (•) below the left side digit of minuend and subtract 8 from 17.

Now, $\qquad$ $17 - 8 = 9$

Now, to subtract 8 from 9, subtract 8 from 8 *ie,* $8 - 8 = 0$

Similarly, to subtract 7 from 3,

$\qquad$ $13 - 7 = 6$

and to subtract 6 from 7.

$\qquad$ $6 - 6 = 0$

Thus, $\qquad$ $7397 - 6788 = 609$

Example 4 *Subtract* 268289 *from* 653901.

Solution $\qquad$
```
6 5 3 9 0 1
  • •   • •
2 6 8 2 8 9
3 8 5 6 1 2
```

To subtract 9 from 1, put a dot (•) below the left side digit of upper value minuend and subtract 9 from 11. *ie,* $11 - 9 = 2$. Now, to subtract 8 from 0, subtract 8 from 9 after putting a dot (•) below 9.

Similarly, $\qquad$ $9 - 2 = 8 - 2 = 6$

$\qquad$ $3 - 8 = 13 - 8 = 5$

$\qquad$ $5 - 6 = 14 - 6 = 8$

and $\qquad$ $6 - 2 = 5 - 2 = 3$

Thus, $\qquad$ $653901 - 268289 = 385612$

Subtraction Using "Nikhilum Navataha Charmam Dashtaha"

For subtraction, Nikhilum sutra is also used but this is particullarly useful if minuend is a multiple of 100. Since the meaning of the vedic sutra "Nikhilum Navataha Charmam Dashtaha" is "All from nine and the last from ten". So, right side is subtracted from 10 and remaining from 9.

To understand this process, follow the following examples.

Example 5 *Subtract* 8732 *from* 10000.

Solution

$$
\begin{array}{r}
1\,0\,0\,0\,0 \\
8\,7\,3\,2 \\
\hline
1\,2\,6\,8 \\
\hline
\end{array}
$$

Subtract 2 from 10 ie, $10 - 2 = 8$
and rest from 9 ie,

$$9 - 3 = 6$$
$$9 - 7 = 2$$
and $$9 - 8 = 1$$
Thus, $$10000 - 8732 = 1268$$

Example 6 *Subtract* 876 *from* 100000.

Solution

$$
\begin{array}{r}
1\,0\,0\,0\,0\,0 \\
8\,7\,6 \\
\hline
9\,9\,1\,2\,4 \\
\hline
\end{array}
$$

Subtract 6 from 10 ie, $10 - 6 = 4$
and rest from 9 ie,

$$9 - 7 = 2$$
$$9 - 8 = 1$$
and $$9 - 0 = 9$$
Thus, $$100000 - 876 = 99124$$

Further Nikhilum sutra can be used for other numbers (ie, except where minuend is not a multiple of 10) but the process is long.

Before studying subtraction using vedic sutra "Nikhilum", we should know about the deficit of a number.

Deficit of a number is also called as Ten's Complement. Deficit of a number is obtained by subtracting the given number from next functional base.

eg, The deficit of 667 is $1000 - 667 = 333$. (Since 1000 is next functional base to 667).

Thus, deficit of a number = functional base – given number.

To find the deficit of a number, subtract last digit from 10 and rests from 9. This is due to vedic sutra "Nikhilum Navataha Charmam Dastaha".

It should be noted in this case if last digit is zero, then subtract first non-zero number from 10 and rests from 9 and put zero after it.

Now, for subtraction using "Nikhilum" sutra, take a deficit of a number (subtrahand) and add it to the another number (minuend), then subtract the last functional base of resultant from the resultant. It should be much clear with help of the following examples.

Example 7   *Subtract* 67 *from* 234.

Solution   Since, subtrahand is 67 whose deficit is $100 - 67$ *ie*, 33.
Now, add 33 to 234. So, $33 + 234 = 267$

Also, last functional base of 67 is 100.

So, resultant number $= 267 - 100 = 167$

Thus, $234 - 67 = 167$.

Example 8   *Subtract* 2876 *from* 3453.

Solution   Since, subtrahand is 2876 whose deficit is 7124.

Now, $3453 + 7124 = 10577$

Also, last functional base of 2876 is 10000. So, result $= 10577 - 10000$

$$= 577$$

Thus, $3453 - 2876 = 577$.

Subtraction of Polynomials

To subtract a polynomial from another polynomial, use the vedic sutra "Paravartya Yojayet". The meaning of this sutra is "Transpose and Apply".

First change the sign of digits in each term of the subtrahand and add that to the corresponding term of the minuend.

Follow the following examples to understand better this process of calculation.

Example 9   *Subtract* $x^4 + 3x^2 + 6x^2 + 7x + 7$ *from* $x^5 - x^3 + 8x^2 + 3$.

Solution

	x^5	x^4	x^3	x^2	x^1	const
$x^5 - x^3 + 8x^2 + 3 \rightarrow$	1	0	$\bar{1}$	8	0	3
$x^4 + 3x^2 + 6x^2 + 7x + 7 \rightarrow$	$\bar{0}$	$\bar{1}$	$\bar{3}$	$\bar{6}$	$\bar{7}$	$\bar{7}$
	1	1	4	2	7	4

$$\begin{pmatrix} \bar{7} + 3 = -7 + 3 = -4 = \bar{4}, \\ 0 + \bar{7} = \bar{7}, 8 + \bar{6} = 8 - 6 = 2, \\ \bar{1} + \bar{3} = -1 - 3 = -4, \\ 0 + \bar{1} = 0 - 1 = \bar{1}, 1 + \bar{0} = 1 - 0 = 1 \end{pmatrix}$$

Thus, required difference is $x^5 - x^4 + 2x^3 + 2x^2 - 7x - 4$.

Example 10   *Subtract* $4x + 2$ *from* $9x + 7$.

Solution

	x	const
$9x + 7 \rightarrow$	9	7
$4x + 2 \rightarrow$	$\bar{4}$	$\bar{2}$
	5	5

$$\begin{pmatrix} 7 + \bar{2} = 7 - 2 = 5 \\ 9 + \bar{4} = 9 - 4 = 5 \end{pmatrix}$$

Thus, required difference is $5x + 5$.

Chapter Practice

Exercise 1

1. Subtract the first number from the second number using "Ekadhikena Poorvena".
   - (i) 35, 62
   - (ii) 632, 931
   - (iii) 9302,13080
   - (iv) 35438,46437
   - (v) 10392, 14293
   - (vi) 25690,29439
   - (vii) 25602, 36499
   - (viii) 323644,663111
   - (ix) 543937,561257
   - (x) 32369060,39403230

2. Subtract the first number from the second number using "Ekanyuneva Poorvena".
   - (i) 1690, 1930
   - (ii) 3260, 3490
   - (iii) 606, 963
   - (iv) 7369, 7978
   - (v) 16493901, 26828916
   - (vi) 3211960, 3212640
   - (vii) 169001, 326400
   - (viii) 21694, 36942
   - (ix) 9216963, 10014790
   - (x) 1029630, 1639410

3. Subtract the first number from the second number using "Nikhilium Navataha Charmam Dashtaha".
   - (i) 90, 100
   - (ii) 63,100
   - (iii) 179,1000
   - (iv) 1490,10000
   - (v) 19568, 30125
   - (vi) 1690, 1783
   - (vii) 9052347,12046035
   - (viii) 735678, 930165
   - (ix) 905265, 1878642
   - (x) 160438, 169032

4. Subtract the first polynomial from the second one using "Paravartya Yojayet".
   - (i) $4x+3, 5x+9$
   - (ii) $7x+4, 15x-4$
   - (iii) $16x^2+15x+4, x^2-1$
   - (iv) $14x^2+3x+1, x^2-1$
   - (v) $29x^2+16x-14, 12x^2+9x$
   - (vi) $x^3+2x^2+3x+9, 4x^3+4x^2+9x+2$
   - (vii) $x^4+x^3+2x+7, x^3+7x^2+7x+9$
   - (viii) $x^4-1, x^5+x^4+x^2+x-1$
   - (ix) $6x^5+2x^3+3x^2+7x+9, x^5+x^3+6x^2+7$
   - (x) $12x^6+1, 14x^5-1$

Exercise 2

1. $(6158-543-111)$ is equal to $\hspace{2cm}$ (OBC Clerk, 09)
   - (a) 5504
   - (b) 5608
   - (c) 5710
   - (d) 5816

2. $(995-618+84)$ is equal to $\hspace{2cm}$ (OBC Clerk, 09)
   - (a) 461
   - (b) 471
   - (c) 481
   - (d) 491

3. If $8153+1492 = x-6175$, then x is equal to $\hspace{1cm}$ (OBC Clerk, 09)
   - (a) 13870
   - (b) 14960
   - (c) 15820
   - (d) 16750

4. $(98678 - 45099 - 10036)$ is equal to   **(Central Bank of India Clerk, 09)**
   (a) 43543   (b) 45343   (c) 44353   (d) 43345

5. $(10354 - 6815 - 1359)$ is equal to   **(Indian Overseas Bank Clerk, 09)**
   (a) 2270   (b) 1940   (c) 1720   (d) None of these

6. If $58321 + 69386 = x + 37098$, then x is equal to   **(Indian Overseas Bank Clerk, 09)**
   (a) 91619   (b) 90609   (c) 92609   (d) 89619

7. If $9879 - x = 1358$, then x is equal to   **(Dena Bank Clerk, 09)**
   (a) 8521   (b) 11273   (c) 7251   (d) 8421

8. $(-31 - 35 - 37 + 18 + 17)$ is equal to   **(Dena Bank Clerk, 09)**
   (a) 68   (b) 103   (c) -138 (d) None of these

9. If $5982 + 1345 + 736 - x = 4588 + 992$, then x is equal to   **(Dena Bank PO, 09)**
   (a) 2485   (b) 2480   (c) 2473   (d) None of these

10. If $8888 + 848 + 88 - x = 7337 + 737$, then x is equal to   **(Canara Bank PO, 09)**
    (a) 1650   (b) 1750   (c) 1550   (d) 1450

Answers

Exercise 1

1. (i) 27   (ii) 299   (iii) 3778   (iv) 10999
   (v) 3901   (vi) 3749   (vii) 10897   (viii) 339467
   (ix) 17320   (x) 7034170

2. (i) 240   (ii) 230   (iii) 357   (iv) 609
   (v) 10335015   (vi) 680   (vii) 157399   (viii) 15248
   (ix) 797827   (x) 609780

3. (i) 10   (ii) 27   (iii) 821   (iv) 8510
   (v) 10557   (vi) 93   (vii) 2993688   (viii) 194487
   (ix) 973377   (x) 8594

4. (i) $x + 6$ (ii) $8x - 8$
   (iii) $-15x^2 - 15x - 5$ (iv) $-13x^2 - 3x - 2$
   (v) $-17x^2 - 7x + 14$ (vi) $3x^3 + 2x^2 + 6x - 7$
   (vii) $-x^4 + 7x^2 + 5x + 2$ (viii) $x^5 + x^2 + x$
   (ix) $-5x^5 - x^3 + 3x^2 - 7x - 2$ (x) $-12x^6 + 14x^5 - 2$

Exercise 2

1. (a)   2. (a)   3. (c)   4. (a)   5. (d)
6. (b)   7. (a)   8. (d)   9. (d)   10. (b)

3 Multiplication

Multiplication is also a fundamental operation in Mathematics. There is a traditional way to multiply the numbers but it is easy to do with the help of the vedic sutra which gives speed.

"Nikhilum Navatha Charmam Dashtaha" and "Urdhva Tiryak" are used to get a easiest way of calculation.

Multiplication Using "Nikhilum" Sutra

"Nikhilum Navataha Charmam Dashtaha" is used to simply the process of multiplication. The meaning of this sutra is "all from nine and last from ten". With the help of this sutra we get the complement of a number which is used for finding the product.

We classified the use of this sutra in the following classes.

(i) When both the numbers are less than the nearest working base

When both the numbers are less than nearest working base, then first find the complements of multiplicand and multiplier, that should be in digits equal to multiplicand and multipliers ie, for the number 97, complement is 3 but it should be written in the form 03. Also, put a negative sign before complement which shows that the number is how much less than the working base. Write corresponding complements against multiplicand and multipliers respectively.

Now, find the product of these complements, the result is right side of resultant. Also, the sum of cross numbers is the left side of resultant. In this process we should be very careful about the carryovers. In the product of single digits number right side will with be single digit and for the product of two digits numbers right side will with be two digits and so on, the remaining carryover will be with left side digit (by adding).

This process will be much clear in the following examples.

Example 1 *Find the product of 5 and 6.*

Solution Complements of 5 and 6 are respectively 5 and 4.

∴

$$\begin{array}{r} 5 \qquad -5 \\ 6 \qquad -4 \\ \hline 1 \quad / \quad 20 \end{array}$$

Now, complements are put against the multiplicand and multiplier respectively with negative sign. Find the product of (–5) and (– 4) which is 20 and cross sum is 5 – 4 or 6 – 5 (= 1). Thus, 20 is left side and 1 is right side of resultant. But left side should be in one digit. So, 2 is added to 1. So, left side is 0 and right side is now 3.

Hence, $5 \times 6 = 30$.

Example 2 *Find the product of 91 and 93.*

Solution Complements of 91 and 93 are respectively 9 and 7.

∴

$$
\begin{array}{r|r}
91 & -09 \\
93 & -07 \\
\hline
84 & 63 \\
\end{array}
$$

Now, complements are put against the numbers with negative sign. Bu be careful here since the numbers are of two digits, so complements should also be of two digits which is made by putting zero before complement.

Find the product of (− 09) and (− 07) which is 63, also cross sum is (93 − 09) or (91 − 07) equal to 84.

Thus, $91 \times 93 = 8463$

Example 3 *Find the product of 995 and 997.*

Solution Complements of 995 and 997 are 005 and 003 respectively.

$$
\begin{array}{r|r}
995 & -005 \\
997 & -003 \\
\hline
992 & 015 \\
\end{array}
$$

Complements are put against numbers with negative sign. Find the product of (−005) and (−003) which is 15 but it should be of three digits, so put one zero before 15. Also, find the cross sum which is (997 − 005) ie, 992.

Thus, $995 \times 997 = 992\,015$

Let two numbers be x and y, then

$$xy = (X - a)(X - b) = X(X - a - b) + ab$$

where X is working base and a and b are complements of x and y respectively.

eg,
$$97 \times 94 = (100 - 3)(100 - 6)$$
$$= 100(100 - 3 - 6) + (3 \times 6)$$
$$= 100 \times 91 + 18$$
$$= 9100 + 18 = 9118$$

and
$$76 \times 86 = (100 - 24)(100 - 14)$$
$$= 100(100 - 24 - 14) + (24 \times 14)$$
$$= 100 \times 62 + 336$$
$$= 6200 + 336 = 6536$$

This may be a special note to find the product in easiest way. But this is useful to the numbers which are near to a working base.

(ii) When both the numbers are greater than the nearest working base

In those cases, in which numbers are greater than the nearest working base, everything is same but the complements of multiplicand and multiplier are put against corresponding numbers with positive sign.

The process will be much clear with help of the following examples.

Example 4 *Multiply* 13 *and* 16.

Solution Since the complements of 13 and 16 are 03 and 06 respectively.

$$\therefore \quad \begin{array}{c|c} 13 & 03 \\ 16 & 06 \\ \hline 19 \quad / & 18 \end{array}$$

Now, complements are put against multiplicand and multiplier with positive sign. Find the product (03) and (06) which is 18. Also, cross sum is $16 + 03 = 19$

Thus, $\qquad 13 \times 16 = 19 / 18 = 208$

Example 5 *Solve* 115×103.

Solution Complements of 115 and 103 are 015 and 03.

$$\begin{array}{c|c} 115 & 015 \\ 103 & 003 \\ \hline 118 \quad / & 045 \end{array}$$

Put complements against the numbers.

Find the product of 15 and 03 which is 45. Also, cross sum is $103 + 15 = 118$. So, right side of resultant is 45 and left side is 118.

Thus, $\qquad 115 \times 103 = 11845$

Example 6 *Solve* 1013×1006.

Solution Complements of 1013 and 1006 are 13 and 6.

$$\begin{array}{c|c} 1013 & 013 \\ 1006 & 006 \\ \hline 1019 \quad / & 078 \end{array}$$

Put Complements against numbers and find the product 13 and 6 which is 78.

and $\qquad$ cross sum $= 1006 + 13 = 1019$.

So, left side of number is 1019 and right side is 078.

Thus, $\qquad 1013 \times 1006 = 1019078$.

Let two numbers be x and y, then
$$xy = (X + a)(X + b)$$
$$= X(X + a + b) + ab$$
where X is working base and a and b are complements of x and y respectively.

eg, $\qquad 102 \times 109 = (100 + 2)(100 + 9)$
$$= 100(100 + 2 + 9) + 2 \times 9$$
$$= 100(111) + 18$$
$$= 11100 + 18$$
$$= 11118.$$

(iii) When one number is less than working base and other is greater than working base

In this case greater number (than working base) has a complement against that with positive sign and other smaller number has a complement against that with negative sign. These sign are used in cross sum and put a bar on the product for right side. All other rules regarding digit surplus, digit deficit etc, will be exactly the same as before.

Example 7 *Solve* 1013×986.

Solution Complements of 1013 and 986 are respectively 13 and –14.

$$
\begin{array}{r}
1013 \qquad 13 \\
986 \qquad -14 \\
\hline
999 \ / \ 182
\end{array}
$$

Here, left side $= 986 + 13$ or $1013 - 14 = 999$

and

$$
\begin{aligned}
\text{right side} &= 13 \times 14 = (10 + 3)(10 + 4) \\
&= 10(10 + 3 + 4) + (3 \times 4) \\
&= 10(17) + 12 \\
&= 170 + 12 = 182.
\end{aligned}
$$

Thus,

$$
\begin{aligned}
1013 \times 986 &= 999 / 182 \\
&= 999 / (1000 - 182) \\
&= 999818.
\end{aligned}
$$

(iv) When the numbers are not nearer to working base

When the numbers are not nearer to working base 10, or multiple of 10. Take a base near the numbers but cross sum (left side of resultant) is multiplied by the number (which is obtained by dividing assumed base by last working base). Here it is noted that this number is an integer.

All other rules will be exactly the same as before.

To understand the process follow the following examples.

Example 8 *Find the product of* 65 *and* 57.

Solution Let base is 60 which is 6 times to the last working base 10. Complements of 65 and 57 are +05 and – 03 respectively.

$$
\begin{array}{r}
65 \qquad + 05 \\
57 \qquad - 03 \\
\hline
62 \ / \ \overline{15} \\
\hline
= 65 - 03 \text{ or } 57 + 5
\end{array}
$$

Left side

$$= 62 \times 6 = 372$$

and right side

$$= \overline{15}$$

Thus,

$$
\begin{aligned}
65 \times 57 &= 372 / \overline{15} \\
&= 370 / (20 - 15) \\
&= 370 / 5 = 3705.
\end{aligned}
$$

Example 9 *Find the product of* 9561 *and* 8997.

Solution Let base is 9000 which is 9 times to the 1000. Complements of 9561 and 8997 are 561 and –3 respectively.

$\therefore$

$$
\begin{array}{r}
9561 \qquad 561 \\
8997 \qquad -3 \\
\hline
9558 \ / \ 1683
\end{array}
$$

$$\therefore \quad \text{Left side} = 9558 \times 9$$
$$= 86022$$
and
$$\text{right side} = 561 \times (\overline{3})$$
$$= \overline{1683}$$
Thus,
$$9561 \times 8997 = 86022 / \overline{1683}$$
$$= 86020 / (2000 - 1683)$$
$$= 86020 / 317$$
$$= 86020317$$

Multiplication Using "Urdhva Triyagbhyam"

The vedic sutra "UrdhvaTriyagbhyam" is used to multiply any numbers and can be used to find the product of any number of numbers.

This method is very general (since applicable to any multiplication), shorter than the conventional method, although longer than the "Nikhilum" method. Its advantage over the conventional method is that it is suitable for mental working. It is based on sutra "Urdhva Triyagbhyam" which means "vertically and cross wise".

In this method we do the calculation from left to right unlike in the conventional method, where we start from right. This enables us to calculate significant digits of the answer prior to the non-significant ones.

We divide this method for these cases.

(i) When numbers are of two digits

Let two numbers are ab and cd.
$$\therefore \quad ab \times cd = (a \times c) / (a \times d + b \times c) / (b \times d)$$

Example 10 *Find the product of 65 and 62.*

Solution
$$65$$
$$\times 62$$
$$\overline{(6 \times 6) / (6 \times 2 + 6 \times 5) / (5 \times 2)} = 36 / 42 / 10$$
$$= 36 / 43 / 0 = 4030$$

Carryovers should be cared by you.

(ii) When numbers are of three digits

Let two numbers are abc and def.
$$\therefore \qquad abc$$
$$\times def$$
$$\overline{(a \times d) / (a \times e + b \times d) / (a \times f + b \times e + c \times d) / (b \times f + c \times e) / (c \times f)}$$

Example 11 *Find the product of 321 and 362.*

Solution
$$321$$
$$\times 362$$
$$\overline{(3 \times 3) / (3 \times 6 + 2 \times 3) / (3 \times 2 + 2 \times 6 + 1 \times 3) / (2 \times 2 + 1 \times 6) / (1 \times 2)}$$
$$= 9 / 24 / 21 / 10 / 2 = 9 / 24 / 22 / 02 = 9 / 26 / 202 = 116202$$

- The same technique can be extended to find product of two 4 digits numbers or two 5 digits numbers. In 4 digits numbers, the product will consist of 7 parts, while in 5 digits numbers the product will consist of 9 parts.
- For decimal numbers, multiply the numbers without decimal and put the decimal at proper position.
- If number of digits are not same in both number, put zeroes in the left in the number with smaller number.

Multiplication of Polynomials Using "Urdhva Triyagbhyam"

The product of two polynomial can be done with the help of the vedic sutra "Urdhva Triyagbhyam".

The process of multiplication using this sutra will be much clear with help of following two examples.

Example 12   *Solve* $(2x + 3)(2x + 9)$.

Solution

Polynomial	x-base	Numbers
$2x + 3$	2	3
$2x + 9$	2	9

Term involving x^2 is $\begin{matrix}2\\2\end{matrix}\Big\uparrow = 2 \times 2 = 4$

$\Rightarrow$ $4x^2$

Term involving x is $\begin{matrix}2\\2\end{matrix}\times\begin{matrix}3\\9\end{matrix} = 2 \times 9 + 2 \times 3 = 24$

$\Rightarrow$ $24x$

and term independent of x is $\begin{matrix}3\\9\end{matrix}\Big\uparrow = 3 \times 9 = 27$

Thus, $(2x + 3)(2x + 9) = 4x^2 + 24x + 27$

Example 13   *Find the product* $(9x^2 + 6x + 5)$ *and* $(4x^2 + 6x + 5)$.

Solution

Polynomial	x-base numbers
$9x^2 + 6x + 5$	9 6 5
$4x^2 + 6x + 5$	4 6 5

Term involving x^4 is $\begin{matrix}9\\4\end{matrix}\uparrow = 9 \times 4 = 36$

$\Rightarrow$ $36x^4$

Term involving x^3 is $\begin{matrix}9\\4\end{matrix}\times\begin{matrix}6\\6\end{matrix} = 9 \times 6 + 6 \times 4$

$ = 54 + 24 = 78$

$\Rightarrow$ $78x^3$

Term involving x^2 is

$$= 9 \times 5 + 6 \times 6 + 4 \times 5$$
$$= 45 + 36 + 20 = 101$$
$$\Rightarrow \qquad 101x^2 .$$

Term involving x is

$$= 6 \times 5 + 6 \times 5$$
$$= 30 + 30 = 60$$
$$\Rightarrow \qquad 60x$$

and term independent of x is $\begin{smallmatrix}5\\5\end{smallmatrix} = 25$

$$\Rightarrow \qquad 25$$

Thus, $\quad (9x^2 + 6x + 5)(4x^2 + 6x + 5) = 36x^4 + 78x^3 + 101x^2 + 60x + 25$

(i) *The above two examples are formulated as*

$$ax + b$$
$$\times cx + d$$
$$\overline{acx^2 + (ad + bc)x + bd}$$

and
$$ax^2 + bx + c$$
$$dx^2 + ex + f$$
$$\overline{adx^4 + (ae + bd)x^3 + (af + be + cd)\,x^2 + (bf + ce)x + cf.}$$

(ii) *If any term contains negative sign that is used properly with coefficient ie,*
   $(2x - 3)$ has 2 and -3 as coefficients.

Chapter Practice

Exercise 1

1. Solve the following using sutra "Nikhilum".
   - (i) 94×98
   - (ii) 98×86
   - (iii) 78×97
   - (iv) 786×998
   - (v) 113×998
   - (vi) 99979×99999
   - (vii) 99.5×0.89
   - (viii) 9.97×0.88
   - (ix) 112×109
   - (x) 10009×10007
   - (xi) 1.901×10.02
   - (xii) 10.15×101.0
   - (xiii) 109×96
   - (xiv) 996×1008
   - (xv) 1027×998
   - (xvi) 1.14×9.2
   - (xvii) 64×56
   - (xviii) 9651×8993
   - (xix) 8451×6253
   - (xx) 334×307

2. Solve the following using sutra "Urdhva Triyagbhyam"
   - (i) 31×49
   - (ii) 33×34
   - (iii) 242×568
   - (iv) 719×888
   - (v) 5.4×5.7
   - (vi) 7.6×0.77
   - (vii) 7500×81
   - (viii) 1.231×5.134
   - (ix) 769×893
   - (x) 99963×99872
   - (xi) 11228×9999
   - (xii) 9651×8993
   - (xiii) 689×343
   - (xiv) 85×97
   - (xv) 94×87
   - (xvi) 989×769
   - (xvii) 334×307
   - (xviii) 114×16
   - (xix) 99×104
   - (xx) 160×149

3. Find the product of polynomials.
   - (i) $(2x + 1)$ and $(3x + 7)$
   - (ii) $(2x + 9)$ and $(3x + 5)$
   - (iii) $(3x + 9)$ and $(6x + 2)$
   - (iv) $(4x^2 + 2x + 1)$ and $(8x^2 + 2x + 5)$
   - (v) $(ax^2 + bx + c)$ and $(cx^2 + dx + e)$
   - (vi) $(6x^2 + 6x + 8)$ and $(4x^2 + 5x + 7)$
   - (vii) $(4x^3 + 2x^2 + 3)$ and $(4x^3 + 7x^2 + 4x)$
   - (viii) $(x^3 + 1)$ and $(x^2 + 1)$
   - (ix) $(x^2 + 1)$ and $(x^2 - 2)$
   - (x) $(x^2 + 5)(x^3 + x - 5)$

4. If cost of one kg of rice is Rs 19.60. How much one has to pay for 9.5 kg of rice ?

5. If rate for construction of 1 cubic meter of brick work is Rs 992, what would be co·ᵢ of 1005 cubic meters of brick work?

6. A space ship is travelling at the speed of 9995 km/h. How much distance v ᵤld it travel in 10004 h?

7. If a vendor purchases 11 carpets for Rs 10000 and sells each carpet for R 990, then how much profit he would make?

8. Ritu has taken a long loan term for purchasing a flat. She has to pay Rs 2·.35 per month to the finance company as installment towards the loan. How much ᵗ ᴊtal money, she will pay over 20 yrs, to the company?

9. A group of 83 students and 7 teachers of a school, goes to science exhibition. If the entrance fee is Rs 75 per student and Rs 150 per teacher, how much total amount in terms of rupees, the group has to give ?

10. If sale price of a saree is Rs 630. If a discount of 14% is given on it, what would be its price?

Exercise 2

1. $(495 \times 38 - 1885)$ is equal to   (OBC Clerk, 09)
   (a) 16695   (b) 16745
   (c) 16885   (d) 16925

2. $(180 \times 18 \times 8 - 8888)$ is equal to   (OBC Clerk, 09)
   (a) 14036   (b) 15048
   (c) 16012   (d) 17032

3. $(555 \times 61 - 25000)$ is equal to   (Central Bank of India Clerk, 09)
   (a) 8855   (b) 8558
   (c) 8585   (d) 8858

4. $(338 \times 97 - 1835)$ is equal to   (Indian Overseas Bank Clerk, 09)
   (a) 30951   (b) 31951
   (c) 29951   (d) 32951

5. $(15 + 150 \times 12)$ is equal to   (Dena Bank Clerk, 09)
   (a) 165   (b) 1980
   (c) 27000   (d) 1815

6. $120 \times (2 + 12)$ is equal to   (Dena Bank Clerk, 09)
   (a) 1680   (b) 252
   (c) 134   (d) 1340

7. $(15 + 15) \times 20$ is equal to   (Dena Bank Clerk, 09)
   (a) 4500   (b) 300
   (c) 315   (d) None of these

8. The product of 995 and 997 is   (Dena Bank Clerk, 09)
   (a) 99015   (b) 992015
   (c) 99215   (d) None of these

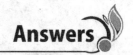

Answers

Exercise 1

1.
(i) 9212	(ii) 8428	(iii) 7566	(iv) 784428
(v) 112774	(vi) 9997800021	(vii) 88.555	(viii) 8.7736
(ix) 12208	(x) 100160063	(xi) 19.04802	(xii) 1025.15
(xiii) 10464	(xiv) 1003968	(xv) 1024946	(xvi) 10.488
(xvii) 3584	(xviii) 86791443	(xix) 52844103	(xx) 102538

2.
(i) 1519	(ii) 1122	(iii) 137456	(iv) 638472
(v) 30.78	(vi) 5.852	(vii) 607500	(viii) 6.319954
(ix) 686717	(x) 9983504736	(xi) 112268772	(xii) 86791443
(xiii) 236327	(xiv) 8245	(xv) 8178	(xvi) 760541
(xvii) 102538	(xviii) 1824	(xix) 10296	(xx) 23840

3.
(i) $6x^2 + 13x + 7$

(ii) $6x^2 + 37x + 45$

(iii) $18x^2 + 60x + 18$

(iv) $32x^4 + 24x^3 + 32x^2 + 12x + 5$

(v) $acx^4 + (ad + bc)x^3 + (ae + bd + c^2)\, x^2 + (be + cd)\, x + ce$

(vi) $24x^4 + 54x^3 + 104x^2 + 82x + 56$

(vii) $16x^6 + 36x^5 + 30x^4 + 20x^3 + 21x^2 + 12x$

(viii) $x^5 + x^3 + x^2 + 1$

(ix) $x^4 - x^2 - 2$

(x) $x^5 + 6x^3 - 5x^2 + 5x - 25$

4. Rs 186.20   **5.** Rs 996960   **6.** 99989980 km   **7.** Rs 890

8. Rs 536400   **9.** Rs 7275   **10.** Rs 541.80

Exercise 2

1. (d)   **2.** (d)   **3.** (a)   **4.** (a)   **5.** (d)

6. (a)   **7.** (d)   **8.** (b)

Division

The vedic methods of division are based on the Sutras "Nikhilum Navataha Charmam Dashtaha", "Paravartya Yojayet" and "Urdhva Triyagbhyam". Urdhva Tiryak sutra is the "crowing gem of all the sutras". The other methods have limitation that they are applicable to a particular class of problems on the other hand, "Urdhva Triyagbhyam" is very general method and quicker compared to our conventional method. But all of these vedic methods of division are illustrated below.

Division Using "Nikhilum" Sutra

The process of division of a number (dividends) by another number (divisor) is split in the following steps or we can say that the calculation is done on the basis of following steps.

First separate extreme right digit or a block of digits of a dividend by drawing a slash equal to number of digits in divisor. This block is known as remainder block and left block is called quotient block.

Step I   First separate extreme right digit or a block of digits of a dividened by drawing a slash equal to number of digits in divisor. This block is known as remainder block and left block is called quotient block.

Step II   Put the sum of digits of first left block, below the right digits block.

Step III   Find the sum of digits of left block except last digit of left block towards right and put this sum below the quotient column and continue the same process upto extreme left digit.

Step IV   Find the sum of numbers of left and right block, the value so obtained in the left part is quotient and rest right part is remainder.

Step V   If the remainder is greater than the divisor, continue the same process in remainder block, upto remainder become less than divisor.

This method will be much clear in the following examples.

        Example 1   *Solve* 4657 ÷ 9.

        Solution

9	4 6 5	7
	5 0	15
	5 1 5	2 2
		2
		2 4
	517	4

∴   Quotient = 517 and remainder = 4

In this method, first we separate extreme right digit 7 by drawing a slash ($\because$ divisor has only one digit). Now, sum of digits of left side $(4+6+5)=15$ put below in right block. Now, put the sum of digit of left block except extreme right digit of left block, below the extreme right digit of left block and continue the same process. Now, find the sum of 465 and 50 which is 515 and also find the sum of 7 and 15 which is 22 but it is greater than divisor. So we continue the same process upto getting a remainder less than divisor.

Example 2   *Solve* $14268 \div 867$.

Solution

$$
\begin{array}{c|c|ccc}
867 & 14 & & 2 & 6 & 8 \\
133 & 1 & & 3 & 3 & \\
\hline
& & & 6 & 6 & 5 \\
& 15 & 1 & 2 & 6 & 3 \\
& & & 1 & 3 & 3 \\
\hline
& 16 & & 3 & 9 & 6 \\
\end{array}
$$

$$10-7=3,\ 9-6=3,\ 9-8=1$$
$$1\times133=133$$
$$1+4=5$$
$$5\times133=665$$
$$1\times133=133$$
$$1+15=16$$

∴   Quotient = 16 and remainder = 396

Division Using "Paravartya Yojayet"

In last sutra it is clear that the application of Nikhilum sutra is suitable when divisor-digits are big, yet this sutra is not useful when the divisor consists of small digits. So, we need a sutra which covers other cases. We found the sutra "Paravartya Yojayet" which means "Transpose and Apply".

This method is suitable if divisor is nearer to the 10 or multiple of 10. In this method we follow the following steps.

Step I   Signs of all digits of divisor except the first digit of divisor towards left are changed.

Step II   One vertical line is drawn separating the digits of dividend in such a way that total digits in right block remain equal to the number of those digits of the divisor whose signs are changed.

Step III   The rest of the process is very much as before.

Which will be clear in the following examples.

Example 3   *Solve* $256 \div 11$

Solution

$$
\begin{array}{c|c|c}
11 & 25 & 6 \\
\overline{1} & \overline{2} & \overline{3} \\
\hline
& 23 & 3 \\
\end{array}
$$

1 is transposed into $\overline{1}$ and written underneath.

2 is brought down, $2 \times \overline{1} = \overline{2}$. Which is written below the next digit 5. $5 + \overline{2} = 3$ gives the next answer digit, $3 \times \overline{1} = \overline{3}$. $6 + \overline{3} = 3$ which gives the remainder.

∴   Quotient $= 23$ and remainder $= 3$

Example 4   *Solve* $23689 \div 112$.

Solution

$$
\begin{array}{r|r|r}
112 & 236 & 89 \\
\hline
\overline{1}\,2 & \overline{2}\,4 & \\
\hline
 & \overline{1}\,2 & \\
\hline
 & \overline{1}\,2 & \\
\hline
211 & 57 &
\end{array}
$$

$2 \times \overline{1}\,2 = \overline{2}\,4$ and this is set below the next two dividend digits 3 and 6.

The second column is added, that is $3 + \overline{2} = 1$, to give the next answer digit.

$1 \times \overline{1}\,2 = \overline{1}\,2$ which is put into the next two columns below 6 and 8. The sum of the third column is $6 + \overline{4} + \overline{1} = 1$ and this is the third answer digit. $1 \times \overline{1}\,2 = \overline{1}\,2$ which is set down below the last two dividend digits. The remainder is added up $9 + \overline{2} = 7$ and $8 + \overline{2} + \overline{1} = 5$.

Hence, quotient $= 211$ and remainder $= 57$

Division Using "Urdhva Triyagbhyam"

Swamiji describes the "Urdhva Triyagbhyam" method and the sutra as the "crowning gem of all the sutras". This method is very general method and quicker compared to our conventional method.

To apply the method we follow the following steps.

Step I   Write the divisor in two parts, separating the parts by a slant line. The right hand part is called as Dhwajanka or the flag digit.

Step II   Write the dividend, in front of the divisor as in the conventional method, but keep the digits well spaced so that we may write the next two lines under them in a more legible way. Divide this number also into two parts by a slant line so that the number of digits on the right hand part are same in both the divisor and the dividend.

Step III   Set up the next two lines for writing the intermediate gross dividend and intermediate actual dividend. Set the space above the dividend for writing the answer (the quotient) as usual.

Now, write the starting two digits of the divisor on the "actual dividend" line.

Step V   Divide this number, by the first digit of the divisor. Write the quotient at its usual place, at the top. Write the remainder, in the "gross dividend" line.

Step VI   Take down the next digit of the main dividend and write it to the right of the remainder of step V. These two digits together make the next gross dividend.

Step VII The actual dividend, however, would be this gross dividend minus the product of the last quotient and the flag digit. Write it down on the "actual dividend" line, exactly below the gross dividend.

Step VIII Divide above difference again by the first digit of the divisor, write the quotient on the top line and remainder on the "gross dividend" line. Pull the next digit of the main dividend to the right of this remainder. Find the actual dividend which is written at the appropriate place.

Step IX Continue this procedure until all the digits of the main dividend are exhausted. The number obtained in the top most line is the quotient and in the actual dividend line after the slant line is the remainder.

Follow the following examples to understand the process.

Example 5   *Solve* 38985 ÷ 73.

Solution   By following the steps in the above method.

```
                          534
              7/3 | 3  8  9  8/5
Gross dividend |       39 38/13
Actual dividend| 3  8  24 29/3
```

∴   Quotient = 534 and remainder = 3

Example 6   *Solve* 56378 ÷ 49.

Solution

```
                          1150
              4/9 | 5  6  3  7/8
Gross dividend |    16 33 47/28
Actual dividend| 5  7  24 2/28
```

∴   Quotient = 1150 and remainder = 28

If the dividend was not completely divisible by the divisor. It is possible, to calculate the quotient in decimal fraction format. So, we have to follow the following steps.

Step I The division process up to finding the integer portion of the quotient is the same as explained earlier. We write divisor and the dividend in two parts as before. The two parts are separated by slant lines.

Step II We then create space for writing gross dividend, actual net dividend and quotient as before.

Step III We divide first two digits by the first digit of the divisor, we write quotient on top of first two digits in place meant for quotient. The remainder we write in gross dividend line. We then pull down the next digit, write it to the right of that remainder which gives gross dividend.

Step IV From this gross dividend we subtract the product of quotient digit and Dhwajanka giving resultant, which we write in the net dividend line. If we wanted the answer in the quotient-remainder form, then our procedure would have been over here. But, we want the answer in decimal fraction form; so, we continue the process of division further.

Step V   We give decimal point after last digit in the quotient, placing it above the slant line of the divisor. Then, we put three additional zeroes to the right of the zero of number. (Three zeroes, because, we want the answer up to three places of decimals.)

Step VI   The net dividend obtained in step IV, is divided by the first digit of the divisor. This gives quotient which is written after the decimal point in the quotient line and above the first zero after the slant line. The remainder is written in the gross dividend line as usual. We then pull down the second zero, to the right of this remainder. The net dividend is obtained as usual, by subtracting product of the quotient and Dhwajanka from gross dividend. This difference is written in the net dividend line.

Step VII The process is continued until all the zeroes to the right of slant line are exhausted. This gives us answer. As we want the answer upto any places of decimals.

Example 7   *Divide 220 by 52 upto 3 places of decimals.*

Solution

```
              04.2308
         5/2 | 22/  0   0   0   0
             | 22/ 20  20  10  40
             |_____
             | 22/ 12  16  04  40
```

∴ Quotient = 04.231

Special Case If divisor is of three digits.

The overall procedure remains same as described before, only intricacy increases. The difference occurs in the calculation of actual dividend from the gross dividend, we follow the following steps.

Step I   Here, we put the slant line in the divisor after two digits from the right. Of course, we could have put the slant line after one digit from right; but, in that case we will have to know the multiplication table for a two digit number. This would defeat the basic nature of vedic mathematics methods, viz, ease of calculation. So, there are two digits in the Dhwajanka.

Step II   As we have put the slant line after two digits from right in the divisor, we have to put the slant line in the dividend also, after two digits from right. The slant line divides the dividend in left part and right part. As before, the left part procedure gives us the quotient, while the right one gives the remainder.

Step III   We put the first digit of the dividend on the actual dividend line and divide it of the divisor. The quotient is written in the quotient line, as usual. The remainder is written in gross dividend line, next digit from the dividend is pulled down and written to the right of it. This makes the gross dividend and the procedure is usual.

Step IV   To calculate the actual dividend, we subtract from gross dividend, the product of earlier quotient and first digit of the Dhwajanka.

Step V   By dividing this actual dividend by the first digit of divisor and with usual procedure, we get quotient and gross dividend. From this gross dividend, we subtract the sum of products of last quotient digit by first digit of Dhwajanka and last-but-one quotient digit by second digit of Dhwajanka.

Step VI   The remaining procedure is similar.

Step VII   Please note that, while calculating the remainder, we assumed zero in the quotient line.

Example 8   *Solve* 7031985 ÷ 823.

Solution   After following the above procedure.

$$
\begin{array}{r|ccccc}
 & \multicolumn{5}{l}{08544} \\
\hline
8/23 & 7 & 0 & 3 & 19/8 & 5 \\
 & 70 & 63 & 71 & 59/18 & 285 \\
\hline
 & 7 & 70 & 47 & 37\ 36/28 & \underline{273}
\end{array}
$$

∴ Quotient = 8544 and remainder = 273

Division of Polynomials

In the procedure of division of a polynomial by another, the vedic sutras "Paravartya Yojayet" and "Urdhva Triyagbhya" are used. The meaning of "Paravartya Yojayet" is 'transpose and apply'. Also, the meaning of "Urdhva Triyagbhyam" is vertical and crosswise. Here, we discuss the application of "Urdhva Triyagbhyam" which is explained in the following example.

Example 9   *Divide* $x^2 + 4x + 5$ *by* $x + 2$.

Solution   Here, x^2 and x are the first term of dividend and divisor, so first term of the quotient is $\dfrac{x^2}{x} = x$.

Now, multiply x by 2 to get $2x$ but we need $4x$, which we can get by multiplying again x by 2 and then adding $2x + 2x = 4x$, so second term of quotient should be 2. Now, to get the value of remainder, multiply second term of quotient with 2, it is 4, so remainder = 1.

Chapter Practice

Exercise

1. Solve the following by using "Nikhilum method".
   - (i) 121 ÷ 88
   - (ii) 1111 ÷ 779
   - (iii) 1555 ÷ 893
   - (iv) 1248 ÷ 987
   - (v) 13103 ÷ 8907
   - (vi) 12034 ÷ 79
   - (vii) 2401 ÷ 76
   - (viii) 1212 ÷ 84
   - (ix) 1313 ÷ 87
   - (x) 19234 ÷ 83

2. Solve the following by using "Paravartya method".
   - (i) 14318 ÷ 13
   - (ii) 399888 ÷ 12
   - (iii) 29694 ÷ 14
   - (iv) 363759 ÷ 12
   - (v) 10569 ÷ 103
   - (vi) 10453 ÷ 102
   - (vii) 12343 ÷ 1112
   - (viii) 13981 ÷ 1363
   - (ix) 281118 ÷ 1003
   - (x) 25953 ÷ 123

3. Solve the following by using "Urdhva Triyagbhyam method".
   - (i) 24743 ÷ 62
   - (ii) 3300 ÷ 34
   - (iii) 785672 ÷ 87
   - (iv) 54 ÷ 57
   - (v) 105.8 ÷ 23
   - (vi) 7667.82 ÷ 88
   - (vii) 62032 ÷ 67
   - (viii) 3.96 ÷ 3.1
   - (ix) 8888 ÷ 72
   - (x) 1231 ÷ 5.13

Solve the following word problems by "Urdhva Triyagbhyam" method.

4. A student has obtained total 1836 marks out of 2700 in an exam. What is her performance in terms of percentage of marks?

5. A car travels a distance of 48.75 km in 45 min. What is its speed expressed in km/h ?

6. A cricket batsman has scored 7567 runs in 63 matches. What is his average run rate ? (Find upto 2 places of decimals.)

7. A businessman purchased goods worth Rs 88000 and sold it for Rs 98650. What was his profit percentage? (Find upto 2 places of decimals.)

8. There are 53 officers of different grades working in a branch office of a company. Their total salary per month is Rs 419000. What is average salary per officer in a month? (Give only the Rupee part, ie, integer part.)

9. In an engineering college, there are 1367 boys and 78 girls. What is the ratio of boys to girls? (Find upto 2 places of decimals, ie, XX.XX boys : 1 girl).

10. How many hours would be required for an aeroplane travelling at a speed of 245 km/h to cover a distance of 1082 km? (Find upto 3 places of decimals.)

Answers

		Quotient	Remainder			Quotient	Remainder
1.	(i)	1	33	(ii)	1		332
	(iii)	1	662	(iv)	1		261
	(v)	1	4196	(vi)	152		26
	(vii)	31	45	(viii)	14		36
	(ix)	15	8	(x)	231		61
2.	(i)	1101	5	(ii)	33324		0
	(iii)	2121	0	(iv)	30313		3
	(v)	102	63	(vi)	102		49
	(vii)	11	111	(viii)	10		351
	(ix)	280	278	(x)	211		0
3.	(i)	399	5	(ii)	97		2
	(iii)	9030	62	(iv)	0.9474		—
	(v)	4.5652	—	(vi)	87.1343		—
	(vii)	925.851	—	(viii)	1.2774		—
	(ix)	123.4444	—	(x)	239.96		—

4. 68% **5.** 65 km/h **6.** 120.11

7. 12.10% **8.** Rs 7905 **9.** 17.52

10. 4.416 h

5 Divisibility

A number is said to be divisible by another number if the remainder is zero, when first number is divided by second number. Now, here are few vedic methods to check the divisiblity of any number. Before studying these methods, first we should know about the osculator. There are two types of osculator as follows

- (i) Positive osculator
- (ii) Negative osculator

Positive Osculators

To find the positive osculator the vedic sutra "Ekadhikena Poorvena is used". To find the Ekadhika follow the following points.

- (i) Ekadhikas of all the divisors ending with 9, 19, 29, 39, ... are 1, 2, 3, 4, ... respectively.
- (ii) Ekadhikas of all the divisors ending with 3, 13, 23, 33, ... are 1, 4, 7, 10, ... respectively.
- (iii) Ekadhikas of all the divisors ending with 7, 17, 27, ... are 5, 12, 19, ... respectively.
- (iv) Ekadhikas of all the divisors ending with 1, 11, 21, ... are 1, 10, 19, ... respectively.

Negative Osculators

Negative osculators can be find in easy way which is explained in the following points.

- (i) The negative osculators of numbers ending with digit 1 like 11, 21, 31 etc, is obtained by leaving the last digit. Thus, negative osculators for 11, 21, 31, ... are 1, 2, 3, ... respectively.
- (ii) The negative osculators of numbers ending with digit 7, first multiply this number by 3 and leave the last digit. This will be required osculator. eg, 17 is multiplied by 3 to get 51, leave 1 (as last digit), the negative osculator is 5.
- (iii) Same as above to get the negative osculators of numbers ending with digit 3, first multiply the number by 7, and remaining process is as above.
- (iv) To get negative osculators of numbers ending with digit 9, first multiply the number by 9 and remaining as above.

To Check Divisibility Using Positive Osculators

To test the divisibility using positive osculators, we follow a simple process of multiplication, osculators and addition which will be clear with help of the following examples.

Example 1 *Check, is* 17649 *is divisible by* 7 ?

Solution Since, osculator of 7 is 5.

$$(7 \times 7 = 49, 4 + 1 = 5)$$

Now, $5 \times 9 = 45, \quad 45 + 4 = 49$

(osculator is multiplied with first digit and resultant is added to next digit to 9 of given number) $5 \times 9 = 45, \quad 45 + 4 = 49, \quad 49 + 6 = 55$

(osculator is multiplied with first digit of last resultant 49 *ie*, 9, remaining digit 4 is added to resultant. This result is added to next digit 6 of given number)

This process is followed upto last digit of given number as follows

$$5 \times 5 = 25, \quad 25 + 5 = 30, \quad 30 + 7 = 37$$
$$5 \times 7 = 35, \quad 35 + 3 = 38, \quad 38 + 1 = 39$$
$$5 \times 9 = 45, \quad 45 + 3 = 48, \quad 48 + 1 = 49$$

Now,

1	1	7	6	4	9
(49)	(39)	(37)	(55)	(49)	

Last osculated value is 49, which is divisible by 7. Thus, the number is divisible by 7.

Example 2 *Test the divisibility of* 1114048 *by* 13.

Solution ∵ Osculator is 4.

$4 \times 8 = 32$	$32 + 4 = 36$	
$4 \times 6 = 24$	$24 + 3 = 27$	$27 + 0 = 27$
$4 \times 7 = 28$	$28 + 2 = 30$	$30 + 4 = 34$
$4 \times 4 = 16$	$16 + 3 = 19$	$19 + 1 = 20$
$4 \times 0 = 0$	$0 + 2 = 2$	$2 + 1 = 3$
$4 \times 3 = 12$	$12 + 1 = 13$	

1	1	1	4	0	4	8
(13)	(3)	(20)	(34)	(27)	(36)	

Since, last osculated value 13 is divisible by 13. So, the given number is divisible by 13.

To Check Divisibility Using Negative Osculators

The procedure of checking divisibility using negative osculator is mentioned in the following examples.

Example 3 *Test the divisibility of* 2248091 *by* 131.

Solution First the digits at even places are marked by (–) from right to left and negative osculator is 13.

2	$\overline{2}$	4	$\overline{8}$	0	$\overline{9}$	1
(0)	(20)	(42)	(13)	(52)	(4)	

$$13 \times 1 = 13, \qquad 13 - 9 = 4$$
$$13 \times 4 = 52, \qquad 52 + 0 = 52$$
$$13 \times 2 = 26, \qquad 26 - 5 = 21, \qquad 21 - 8 = 13$$
$$13 \times 3 = 39, \qquad 39 - 1 = 38, \qquad 38 + 4 = 42$$
$$13 \times 2 = 26, \qquad 26 - 4 = 22, \qquad 22 - 2 = 20$$
$$13 \times 0 = 0, \qquad 0 + 2 = 2, \qquad 2 - 2 = 0$$

In this method, bared number should be subtracting in place of addition (as in last method) and resultant remaining digits except last digit should be subtracted.

Since, last osculated value is 0. So, the given number is divisible by 13.

Example 4 *Test the divisibility of 6005746 by 67.*

Solution Since, osculator of 67 is 20.

$$\begin{array}{ccccccc} 6 & \overline{0} & 0 & \overline{5} & 7 & \overline{4} & 6 \\ & (-134) & (-7) & (70) & (104) & (116) & (116) \end{array}$$

Now,

$$20 \times 6 = 120, \qquad 120 - 4 = 116$$
$$20 \times 6 = 120, \qquad 120 - 11 = 109, \qquad 109 + 7 = 116$$
$$20 \times 6 = 120, \qquad 120 - 11 = 109, \qquad 109 - 5 = 104$$
$$20 \times 4 = 80, \qquad 80 - 10 = 70, \qquad 70 + 0 = 70$$
$$20 \times 0 = 0, \qquad 0 - 7 = -7, \qquad -7 + 0 = -7$$
$$20 \times 7 = 140, \qquad 140 + 0 = 140, \qquad -140 + 6 = (-134)$$

Since, 134 is divisible by 67. Thus, the given number is divisible by 67.

Chapter Practice

Exercise

1. **Test the divisibility of the following numbers by using positive osculator.**
   - (i) 668868 by 17
   - (ii) 411723 by 23
   - (iii) 3380246 by 37
   - (iv) 88666326 by 189
   - (v) 5293240096 by 139
   - (vi) 79158435267 by 229
   - (vii) 6056200566 by 283
   - (viii) 739260251 by 347
   - (ix) 8673117259 by 359
   - (x) 885648437 by 367

2. **Test the divisibility of the following numbers by using negative osculator.**
   - (i) 36578684 by 81
   - (ii) 1685159 by 119
   - (iii) 168540054 by 53
   - (iv) 3104305 by 79
   - (v) 4902228096 by 433
   - (vi) 5188888837 by 467
   - (vii) 2093172670510192 by 991
   - (viii) 47946654391 by 421
   - (ix) 147932463 by 391
   - (x) 14724934560 by 371

Answers

1.
   - (i) No
   - (ii) Yes
   - (iii) Yes
   - (iv) Yes
   - (v) Yes
   - (vi) Yes
   - (vii) Yes
   - (viii) Yes
   - (ix) Yes
   - (x) Yes

2.
   - (i) No
   - (ii) Yes
   - (iii) No
   - (iv) Yes
   - (v) No
   - (vi) Yes
   - (vii) Yes
   - (viii) No
   - (ix) No
   - (x) No

6

Square and Square Root

Square of any number means that number is multiplied by itself to get a new number. We have studied some method of multiplication so, the square of any number is further extension of these methods. There are various methods to find the square of numbers but some of them have their own limits.

Square Using Yavadunam Method

The vedic sutra 'Yavadunam Tavadunikritya Vargancha Yojayet' (यावद्धनं तावद्नीकृत्य वर्ग च योजयेत्) which means "whatever the deficiency, lesson by that amount and set up the square of the deficiency."

Case I

This sutra is used when the number is near to the base. Follow the following steps to find the square of a number.

Step I First find the deficet of number from nearer base.

Step II Subtract this base from the number this makes the left block of resultant.

Step III Square the deficit number which have equal number of digits as the base. This makes the right block of resultant.

Be careful in case of carryovers.

Example 1 *Find the square of* 96.

Solution Nearest base is 100.

∴ Deficit of the number from 100 is 4.

Left block of resultant $= 96 - 4 = 92$

and right block of resultant $= (4)^2 = 16$

Thus, $(96)^2 = 92/16 = 9216$

Example 2 *Find the square of* 9893.

Solution Nearest base is 10000.

∴ Deficit from 10000 is 107.

Left block of resultant $= 9893 - 107 = 9786$

and right block of resultant $= (107)^2 = 11449$

(This block will have only four digits since base has 4 zeroes)

∴ $(9893)^2 = 9786/11449 = 9786/1449 = 97871449$

Case II

This case has the numbers which are surplus from base value. The following steps have to follow to find a square of a number.

Step I Find the surplus of the number from the nearest base.

Step II Add this surplus to the number. Remaining procedure is same as in case I.

Example 3 *Find the square of* 107.

Solution Nearest base is 100.

∴ Surplus of the number $= 107 - 100 = 7$

Left block of resultant $= 107 + 7 = 114$

and right block of resultant $= (7)^2 = 49$

Thus, $(107)^2 = 114/49 = 11449$

Example 4 *Find the square of* 1015.

Solution Nearest base is 1000.

∴ Surplus from $1000 = 1015 - 1000 = 15$

Left block of resultant $= 1015 + 15 = 1030$

and right block of resultant $= (15)^2 = 225$

Thus, $(1015)^2 = 1030/225 = 1030225$

Case III

When the surplus or deficit is a vary large value from nearest base. To make a easy calculation, we take a base nearer to the given number and follow the following steps to make a calculation.

Step I Take a base which is a multiple of nearer base.

Step II Find the surplus (or deficit).

Step II Add (or subtract) this surplus (or deficit) to the given number, which makes left block.

Step IV Square surplus (or deficit) which makes right block of resultant.

Step V Multiply those numbers in left block which is obtained by multiple of base.

Example 5 *Find the square of* 29.

Solution Nearest base is 30 which is three times of 10.

Deficit of number $= 30 - 29 = 1$

Left block of resultant $= 3 \times (29 - 1) = 3 \times 28 = 84$

Right block of resultant $= 1^2 = 1$

Thus, $(29)^2 = 84/1 = 841$

"Square Using Ekadhikena Poorvena"

The vedic sutra "Ekadhikena Poorvena" is used in this method which means "By one more than the one before." But this method has limitations ie,. This method is useful for all those numbers which end with digit 5.

The method is as follows.

Let number be $x5$, then its square is $x(x + 1) / 25$.

Example 6 *Find the square of 135.*

Solution $(135)^2 = (13 \times 14) / 5^2$

$$= 182 / 25 = 18225$$

Square Using "Anurupyena"

The vedic sutra "Anurupyena" is used in this method which means 'proportionately'. This method also have its limitations. This method is useful for all those numbers which are of two or three digits numbers.

For Two Digits Numbers

Let number be xy.

$\therefore$ $(xy)^2 = x^2 | 2 \times x \times y | y^2$

For Three Digits Numbers

Let number be xyz.

$\therefore$ $(xyz)^2 = (xy)^2 | 2 \times (xy) \times z | z^2$

or $x^2 | 2 \times x \times (yz) | (yz)^2$

Example 7 *Find the square of 64.*

Solution $(64)^2 = 6^2 | 2 \times 6 \times 4 | 4^2$

$$= 36 | 48 | 16$$
$$= 36 | 49 | 6 = 4096$$

Example 8 *Find the square of 113.*

Solution $(113)^2 = (11)^2 | 2 \times 11 \times 3 | 3^2$

$$= 121 | 66 | 9$$
$$= 12\,7\,69$$

Example 9 *Find the square of 715.*

Solution $(715)^2 = (7)^2 | 2 \times 7 \times 15 | (15)^2$

$$= 49 | 210 | 225$$
$$= 49 | 212 | 25$$
$$= 511225$$

Square Using "Dwandwa Yoga"

This method is names is Duplex method, before studying this method we should know about duplex of any number.

Duplex of a is $\overset{a}{\underset{a}{\big|}} = a \times a$

Duplex of ab is $\times = a \times b + a \times b$

Duplex of abc is

$$\begin{matrix} a & b & c \\ & \times & \\ a & b & c \end{matrix} = a \times c + b \times b + a \times c$$

eg, Duplex of 128 is

$$\begin{matrix} 1 & 2 & 8 \\ & \times & \\ 1 & 2 & 3 \end{matrix} = 1 \times 8 + 2 \times 2 + 1 \times 8$$

$$= 8 + 4 + 8 = 20$$

The same procedure is extended for numbers with more digits.

Once the process of finding the duplex is clear, finding square of number is easy. Let us denote duplex by D and duplex of a by $D(a)$.

Now,

$$a^2 = D(a)$$
$$(ab)^2 = D(a) \,|\, D(ab) \,|\, Db$$
$$(abc)^3 = D(a) \,|\, D(ab) \,|\, D(abc) \,|\, D(bc) \,|\, D(c)$$

The same procedure is extended for numbers with 4 or more digits.

Example 10 *Find the square of* 317.

Solution

$$(317)^2 = D(3) \,|\, D(31) \,|\, D(317) \,|\, D(17) \,|\, D(7)$$
$$= 9 \,|\, 2(3 \times 1) \,|\, 2(3 \times 7) + (1 \times 1) \,|\, 2(1 \times 7) \,|\, 49$$
$$= 9 \,|\, 6 \,|\, 43 \,|\, 14 \,|\, 49$$
$$= 9 \,|\, 6 \,|\, 43 \,|\, 18 \,|\, 9$$
$$= 96 \,|\, 44 \,|\, 89$$
$$= 100489$$

Example 11 *Find the square of* 75.

Solution

$$(75)^2 = D(7) \,|\, D(75) \,|\, D(5)$$
$$= 49 \,|\, 2 \times (7 \times 5) \,|\, 25$$
$$= 49 \,|\, 70 \,|\, 25$$
$$= 56 \,|\, 2 \,|\, 5$$
$$= 5625$$

Square Root

Square root of any number means to get a number which is multiplied by itself gives the given number. In the conventional method of finding the square root, the divisor goes on becoming larger in each step. This increases the calculation time as well as the complexity. Before studying about square root we should know some points.

(i) For finding out square root, we have to arrange the given number in two digits groups starting from right to left. If there are odd numbers of digits, then the left most group will contain one digit only. The number of digits in the square root can also be found by counting these digit groups.

(ii) The square root of a number with 'n' digits will contain $\dfrac{n}{2}$ or $\dfrac{n+1}{2}$ digits.

(iii) The square of any integer must end with either 0, 1, 4, 5, 6 or 9. It cannot end with 2, 3, 7, or 8.

(iv) A number cannot be an exact square, if it ends with an odd number of zeroes.

The method of finding square root, involved the steps, which is explained in the following example.

Example 12   *Find the square root of* 529.

Solution

		2/3	
Gross	5/2	9	
Net	1/2	09	
	/2	0	

(i)   Divide the given number into groups of two digits starting from right. Here, the right-most group consists of two digits 2 and 9 and the remaining group consists of single digit 5. (If somebody insists upon exactness of our definition of 'two digit groups', then consider this last group as 05.). As two groups are there, we know that there would be two digits in the integer part of the square root of 529.

(ii) Set up a table as shown in the figure above, similar to the one we used for division process.

(iii) Here, write 529 with digits well spaced apart in the dividend position. Draw a slant line after the first group (of single digit 5) from left, separating it from rest of the number.

(iv) We are now ready to find out the first digit of the answer. This is to be written above the first (left-most) group, in the quotient line. This number should be largest single-digit number whose square is less than or equal to the number in the first group of the dividend. In the present case the dividend number is 5. There are two single-digit numbers 1 and 2, whose squares are less than 5, We choose the largest among them and write it. So, we write 2 in the quotient line, above 5. We also draw a slant line after this digit in the quotient line.

(v) From the first digit of the square root (answer) calculated in the previous step, we get the divisor for the rest of the process. It is double of the first answer digit. In the present case, double of 2, that is 4 would act as divisor for rest of the process. Write this 4 in the position of the divisor.

(vi) Subtract square 4 of the first quotient digit from the first group number 5 and write the remainder 1, in the gross dividend line. This is to be written below the first digit of the dividend number to the right of slant line. Now, take down the first digit 2 of the right part of the dividend and write it in front of the remainder 1 on the gross line. The gross dividend now is 12. For the first digit of the right part of the dividend, the net dividend is same as the gross dividend. So, simply write down this 12 in the net or actual dividend line also.

(vii) Divide this net dividend 12 by the divisor 4. Write down the quotient 3 after the slant line in the quotient line. Write the remainder 0 on the gross dividend line below the second digit 9 of the right part of the dividend. Take down this 9 and write it in front of the 0 on the gross dividend line making the gross dividend as 9.

(viii) The net dividend is gross dividend minus the *duplex* of the quotient part to the right of slant line. Here, the quotient to the right of slant line is 3. Duplex of 3 is 9. Thus, net dividend is 9 minus 9, that is 0. We write this in the net dividend line. As there are no further digits in the dividend and 0 in the net dividend, out process is over.

The square root is the number in the quotient line, that is 23.

Now, know the procedure for larger numbers which also explained in the following example.

Example 13 *Find the square root of* 16384.

Solution

	1/28.0 (Quotient)			
2	1/6	3	8	4
Gross	06	23	38	64
Net	06	19	06	0

(i) Divide the given number into two-digit groups starting from right. Here, the groups would be 1,63 and 84. This tells us that there would be three digits in the integer portion of the square root. In the present problem, this knowledge is significant.

(ii) Set up a chart similar to the division by *Urdhwa-Tiryag* process and write the given number with digits spaced well apart in the dividend line. Draw a slant line after the first group, which in the present case consists of single digit 1.

(iii) Write the first digit of the answer (square root) on the quotient line. This would be largest such single digit number that its square is less than or equal to the first group of the dividend. In the present case, such number is 1 and we write it in the quotient line above the 1 of the dividend. We also draw a slant line in the quotient line above the one in the dividend line.

(iv) The divisor for the rest of the process would be double of this quotient digit, in the present problem, it is 2 and is written in the usual place for divisor.

(v) Subtract square of the quotient digit 1 from the first group of the dividend. It is 1 minus 1, that is 0. Write this remainder 0 in the gross dividend line below the first digit 6 of the right part of the dividend. Pull down that 6 and write it on he gross dividend line, in front of the 0. The gross dividend is now 06, *ie*, 6. For the first digit of the dividend to the right of slant line, the gross and net dividend are same. So, write this 6 on the net dividend line also, as it is.

(vi) Divide that net dividend 6 by the divisor 2, write the quotient 2 after the slant line in quotient and write the remainder 2 on the gross dividend line below the second digit 3 of the part of the dividend after the slant line. (*Hold your surprise and doubt about the fact that, here, the quotient should be 3 and remainder 0, until the reading of next point ! After that the doubt will vanish!*)

(vii) Pull down the 3 in the dividend line and write it in front of the remainder 2 in the gross dividend line, making the gross dividend as 23. The net dividend is gross dividend minus the duplex of the quotient to the right of slant line. Here, the number of the right of slant line in the quotient is 2. Its duplex is 4. So, the net dividend is 23 minus, that is 19. This 19 is written on the net dividend line below 23 of the gross dividend line. Note that if we had taken the quotient to be 3 and the remainder 0 in the last step, the gross dividend would have been 3 only. Subtracting 9 (duplex of quotient 3) from this gross dividend would give us negative net dividend. This would complicate the procedure terribly. So, we avoid it by taking the wise decision in the last step.

(viii) Divide the net dividend 19 by the divisor 2, write the quotient 8 on the quotient line and the remainder 3 on the gross dividend line below the third digit 8 of the right part of the dividend.

(ix) Pull down this 8 and write it in front of the remainder 3 on the gross dividend line, making the gross dividend 38. The net dividend is gross dividend minus the duplex of the number to the right of slant line in the quotient. This number is 28 right now and its duplex is $2 \times 2 \times 8 = 32$. Subtracting 32 from the gross dividend 38, we get the net dividend as 6.

(x) Divide this net dividend 6 by the divisor 2, write quotient 0 on the quotient line and the remainder 6 on the gross dividend line below the last digit 4 of the dividend. Pull down this 4 and write it on the gross dividend line in front of the remainder 6, making the gross dividend as 64. To get the net dividend, subtract from this 64, the duplex of 280 (the number to the right of slant line in the quotient) that is $8^2 + 2 \times 2 \times 0 = 64$. The net dividend is 0 and the division process stops.

(xi) You may be tempted to assume that square root of 16384 is 1280, but, we have estimated the number of digits in the integer portion of the square root to be 3 (*see step* 1). So, put decimal point after three digits in the answer making it 128.0. As 128.0 is nothing but 128, we say that the answer is 128.

The procedure for finding square roots of non-exact squares is same as above. Only thing to be done more carefully is placement of decimal point which was some what obvious in earlier cases. If we want to find the answer to up to more number of decimal places, we have to add extra zeroes at the end of the given numbers.

Chapter Practice

Exercise 1

1. Find the square of the following numbers using "Yavadunam Method".
   (i) 94   (ii) 96   (iii) 798   (iv) 9895
   (v) 36   (vi) 110   (vii) 10040   (viii) 1013
   (ix) 37   (x) 49   (xi) 34   (xii) 99998
   (xiii) 66049   (xiv) 1225   (xv) 8970

2. Find the square of the following numbers using "Ekadhikena Poorvena".
   (i) 25   (ii) 35   (iii) 65   (iv) 95
   (v) 185   (vi) 205   (vii) 5095   (viii) 9995
   (ix) 10005   (x) 985

3. Find the square of the following numbers using "Anurupyena".
   (i) 46   (ii) 114   (iii) 816   (iv) 460
   (v) 717   (vi) 520   (vii) 69   (viii) 215
   (ix) 7432   (x) 815

4. Find the square of the following numbers using "Dwandwa-Yoga".
   (i) 3014   (ii) 567   (iii) 723   (iv) 347
   (v) 215   (vi) 84029   (vii) 6416   (viii) 210
   (ix) 639   (x) 5509

5. Find the square root of the following numbers.
   (i) 755   (ii) 258   (iii) 3000   (iv) 7352
   (v) 13789   (vi) 9412624   (vii) 1172889 ·   (viii) 4986289
   (ix) 611524   (x) 28224   (xi) 7921   (xii) 5329
   (xiii) 290521   (xiv) 707281   (xv) 8652

Exercise 2

1. $(71)^2$ is equal to   **(OBC Bank Clerk, 09)**
   (a) 5476   (b) 5041   (c) 5329   (d) 4761

2. $(2.5)^2$ is equal to   **(OBC Bank Clerk, 09)**
   (a) 62.5   (b) 0.0625   (c) 6.25   (d) 0.625

3. $(16)^2 + (16)^2$ is equal to   **(OBC Bank Clerk, 09)**
   (a) 512   (b) 256   (c) 4096   (d) 65536

4. If $9408 \div \sqrt{x} = 336$, then x is equal to   **(OBC Bank Clerk, 09)**
   (a) 676   (b) 28   (c) 26   (d) 784

5. If $1254 + 1147 = x^2$, then x is equal to   **(OBC Bank Clerk, 09)**
   (a) 41   (b) 49   (c) 43   (d) 47

6. If $\sqrt{x} + 25 = \sqrt{5329}$ **(OBC Bank Clerk, 09)**
   (a) 2304   (b) 48   (c) 46   (d) 2116

7. What is the least number to be added to 3333 to make it a perfect square ?
   (a) 31   (b) 84   **(OBC Bank Clerk, 09)**
   (c) 78   (d) 57

8. If $\sqrt{x} - 18 = \sqrt{1444}$, then x is equal to   (Central Bank of India Clerk, 09)
   (a) 441   (b) 3136   (c) 400   (d) 484

9. If $79296 \div \sqrt{x} = 112 \times 12$, then x is equal to   (Central Bank of India Clerk, 09)
   (a) 3481   (b) 3721   (c) 3969   (d) 3249

10. If $(51)^2$ is added to the square of a number, the answer so obtained is 15826. What is the number ?   (Central Bank of India Clerk, 09)
    (a) 115   (b) 114   (c) 116   (d) 113

11. If $48096 \div \sqrt{x} = 167 \times 9$, then x is equal to   (Indian Overseas Bank Clerk, 09)
    (a) 1646   (b) 1432   (c) 1024   (d) 1208

12. If $\sqrt{x} + 28 = \sqrt{1681}$, then x is equal to   (Indian Overseas Bank Clerk, 09)
    (a) 13   (b) 225   (c) 169   (d) 15

13. What is the least number to be added to 8200 to make it a perfect square ?
                                                              (Indian Overseas Bank Clerk, 09)
    (a) 81   (b) 100   (c) 264   (d) 154

14. If $(49)^2$ is added to the square of a number, the answer so obtained is 9125. What is the number ?   (Indian Overseas Bank Clerk, 09)
    (a) 6724   (b) 95   (c) 4624   (d) 82

15. If $(64)^2 \div 8^2 = x^2$, then x is equal to   (Dena Bank Clerk, 09)
    (a) 64   (b) 62   (c) 4   (d) 8

16. $\sqrt{(13)^4}$ is equal to   (Dena Bank Clerk, 09)
    (a) 520   (b) 169   (c) 28561   (d) 14280

17. $(2704)^{1/2}$ is equal to   (Dena Bank Clerk, 09)
    (a) 1352   (b) 676   (c) 52   (d) 338

18. $\dfrac{\sqrt{4096} \times 56}{764 - 652}$ is equal to   (SBI Clerk, 09)
    (a) 36   (b) 48   (c) 32   (d) 44

19. If $(94)^2 + x^2 = (145)^2 - (56)^2 - 3869$, then x is equal to   (Dena Bank PO, 09)
    (a) 5184   (b) 72   (c) 84   (d) 7056

20. If $2432 \div x = \sqrt{23104}$, then x is equal to   (Canara Bank PO, 09)
    (a) 12   (b) 14   (c) 18   (d) 16

21. If $x^2 + (123)^2 = (246)^2 - (99)^2 - 2462$, then x is equal to   (Canara Bank PO, 09)
    (a) 184   (b) 186   (c) 182   (d) 180

22. If $[(84)^2 \div 28 \times 12] \div 24 = 7 \times x$, then x is equal to   (Canara Bank PO, 09)
    (a) 18   (b) 17   (c) 19   (d) 21

23. If $\sqrt{x} = (88 \times 42) \div 16$, then x is equal to   (IDBI Officer, 07)
    (a) 3696   (b) 39660   (c) 43163   (d) 53361

24. If $\sqrt{\sqrt{2500} + \sqrt{961}} = x^2$, then x is equal to   (Central Bank of India PO, 06)
    (a) 81   (b) 3   (c) 9   (d) 6561

25. If $\sqrt{915849} + \sqrt{795664} = x^2$, then x is equal to   (UBI PO, 09)
    (a) 1849   (b) 79   (c) 43   (d) 37

26. Square root of 117649 is   (Mat, 00)
    (a) 347   (b) 343   (c) 353   (d) 357

27. The value of $\sqrt{248 + \sqrt{52 + \sqrt{144}}}$ is   (SSCLDC, 04)

    (a) 14   (b) 16   (c) 18   (d) 16.6

28. What should come in the place of question mark (?) in the following equation ?

$$\frac{28}{?} = \frac{?}{112}$$

    (a) 70   (b) 56   (c) 48   (d) 64

29. If $x = 15$ and $y = 20$, then $\sqrt{x^2 + y^2}$ is equal to

    (a) $\sqrt{(15 + 20)^2}$ (b) 35   (c) 625   (d) 25

30. Each student in a class bought roses equal to the total number of students in that class. The total number of roses collected in the class was 576. What could be the total number of students in that class ?

    (a) 23   (b) 24   (c) 25   (d) 26

Answers

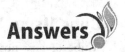

Exercise 1

1.   (i) 8836   (ii) 9216   (iii) 636804   (iv) 97515625
      (v) 1296   (vi) 12100   (vii) 100801600   (viii) 1026169
      (ix) 1369   (x) 2401   (xi) 1156   (xii) 9999600004
      (xiii) 4362470401   (xiv) 1500625   (xv) 80460900

2.   (i) 625   (ii) 1225   (iii) 4225   (iv) 9025
      (v) 34225   (vi) 42025   (vii) 25959025   (viii) 99900025
      (ix) 100100025   (x) 970225

3.   (i) 2116   (ii) 12996   (iii) 665856   (iv) 211600
      (v) 514089   (vi) 270400   (vii) 4761   (viii) 46225
      (ix) 55234624   (x) 664225

4.   (i) 9084196   (ii) 321489   (iii) 522729   (iv) 120409
      (v) 46225   (vi) 7060872841   (vii) 41165056   (viii) 44100
      (ix) 408321   (x) 30349081

5.   (i) 27.4773   (ii) 16.0624   (iii) 54.7722   (iv) 85.7438
      (v) 117.4266   (vi) 3068   (vii) 1083   (viii) 2233
      (ix) 782   (x) 168   (xi) 89   (xii) 73
      (xiii) 539   (xiv) 841   (xv) 29.4143

Exercise 2

   1. (b)   2. (c)   3. (a)   4. (d)   5. (b)
   6. (a)   7. (a)   8. (b)   9. (a)   10. (a)
11. (c)   12. (c)   13. (a)   14. (d)   15. (d)
16. (b)   17. (c)   18. (c)   19. (b)   20. (d)
21. (c)   22. (a)   23. (d)   24. (b)   25. (c)
26. (b)   27. (b)   28. (b)   29. (d)   30. (b)

7   Cube and Cube Root

Cube of a number means a number is multiplied to itself three times. To find the cube vedic sutra. "Yavadunam Tavadunikritya Vargancha Yojayet" and "Anurupyena" are used.

Cube Using Yavadunam Method

Cube of any number nearer to its base can be calculated using vedic sutra "Yavadunam Tavadunikritya Varganicha Yojayet" (यावद्धनं तावद्नी कृत्य वर्ग च योजयेत्) which means "whatever the deficiency, lesson by that amount and set up the square of the deficiency". To find the cube using this method, the following steps should be followed.

Step I   Find the deficit or surplus from the base value, double it and add this result to the given number which gives left block of resultant.

Step II   Now, find the deficit or surplus of new obtained number and multiply it with initial deficit or surplus, which gives middle block a resultant.

Step III   Find the cube of initial deficit or surplus value, which gives right block of resultant.

The method of finding cube will be much clear in the following examples.

Example 1 *Find cube of* 107.

Solution   Surplus is 7.

$\therefore$ Left block of resultant $= 7 \times 2 + 107$

$$= 121$$

and   surplus of new number $= 21$

$\therefore$ Middle block of resultant $= 21 \times 7 = 147$

and   right block of resultant $= (7)^3 = 343$.

Hence, $(107)^3 = 121 / 147 / 343$

$$= 121 / 150 / 43$$

$$= 1225043$$

Example 2 *Find the cube of* 998.

Solution $\because$ Nearest base is 1000 and deficit is 2.

$\therefore$ Left block of resultant $= -2 \times 2 + 998 = 994$

and   surplus of new number $= -6$

$\therefore$ Middle block of resultant $= (-2)(-6) = 12$

and   right block of resultant $= (-2)^3 = -8$

Since, total zeroes in base value are three, so three digits will be allowed at every place.

Hence, $(998)^3 = 994/012/-8$

$$= 994/011/(1000-8)$$

$$= 994/011/992 = 994011992$$

Cube Using Anurupyena Method

In cubing numbers we use vedic sutra "Anurupyena" which means "proportionality". Following steps are to be followed.

For Two Digits Numbers

Let number be xy.

$\therefore$ $(xy)^3 = x^3 / 3x^2 y / 3xy^2 / y^3$

And for three digits numbers

Let number be xyz.

$$(xyz)^3 = (xy)^3 / 3(xy)^2 z / 3(xy) z^2 / z^3$$

Example 3   *Find the cube of 57.*

Solution $(57)^3 = 5^3 / 3 \times 5^2 \times 7 / 3 \times 5 \times 7^2 / 7^3$

$$= 125/525/735/343$$

$$= 125/525/769/3$$

$$= 125/601/93$$

$$= 185/193$$

$$= 185193$$

Example 4   *Find the cube of 112.*

Solution $(112)^3 = (11)^3 / 3 \times (11)^2 \times 2 / 3 \times 11 \times 2^2 / 2^3$

$$= 1331/726/132/8$$

$$= 1331/739/2/8$$

$$= 1404928.$$

This method or formulae can be extend to four or more digits numbers.

Cube Root

Cube root of a number means if the resultant is multiplied three times to itself gives the given number. But finding a cube root is not an easy way. We can find the cube root using "Anurupyena" only for simple numbers but it is a complicated case. Follow the following steps on remembering these two formulae.

$$(xy)^3 = x^3 / 3x^2 y / 3xy^2 / y^3$$

and $(xyz)^3 = (xy)^3 / 3(xy)^2 z / 3(xy)z^2 / z^3$

Step I   First divide the given number in blocks each of three digits from right.

Step II   The number of blocks decide the number of digits in cube root *ie*, if there are two blocks, then cube root has two digits.

Step III   Find the cube root of unit's place digit of right block and assume it equal to y. Also, find the cube of a number nearest to next block and assume it equal to x and so on.

Step IV   Now, use formulae from right to subtract from the given number.
This method will be much clear in the following examples.

Example 5   *Find the cube root of* 357911.

Solution $\overline{357}\,\overline{911}$

Let $y = 1^{1/3} = 1$ and since, cube of 7 is nearer to 347. Thus, $x = 7$.

Now, subtract y^3 from the number.

$$\therefore \qquad\qquad \begin{array}{r} 3\ 5\ 7\ 9\ 11 \\ -\ 1 \\ \hline 3\ 5\ 7\ 9\ 10 \end{array}$$

Now, subtract $3xy^2$ leaving last zero.

$$\begin{array}{r} 3\ 5\ 7\ 9\ 1 \\ 2\ 1 \\ \hline 3\ 5\ 7\ 7\ 0 \end{array}$$

Now, subtract $3x^2y$ leaving last zero.

$$\begin{array}{r} 3\ 5\ 7\ 7 \\ 1\ 4\ 7 \\ \hline 3\ 4\ 3\ 0 \end{array}$$

Now, subtract x^3 leaving last zero.

$$\begin{array}{r} 3\ 4\ 3 \\ 3\ 4\ 3 \\ \hline 0\ 0\ 0 \end{array}$$

Hence, cube root of $357911 = 71$.

Example 6   *Find the cube root of* 1685159.

Solution $\overline{1}\,\overline{685}\,\overline{159}$

Since, the given number has three blocks.

Let $\qquad\qquad\qquad z = 9$
$\qquad\qquad\qquad\qquad y = 1$
and $\qquad\qquad\qquad x = 1$

Now, subtract z^3 from given number.

$$\begin{array}{r} 16\ 85\ 159 \\ 729 \\ \hline 16\ 8\ 4430 \end{array}$$

Now, subtract $3z^2y$ from resultant number leaving zero.

$$\begin{array}{r} 16\ 8\ 443 \\ 243 \\ \hline 16\ 8\ 200 \end{array}$$

Now, subtract $z(z^2x + zy^2)$

$$
\begin{array}{r}
16\ 8\ 20 \\
2\ 70 \\
\hline
16\ 5\ 50
\end{array}
$$

Now, subtract $y^3 + 6xyz$

$$
\begin{array}{r}
16\ 55 \\
55 \\
\hline
16\ 00
\end{array}
$$

Now, subtract $3(x^2z + y^2x)$

$$
\begin{array}{r}
160 \\
-30 \\
\hline
130
\end{array}
$$

Now, subtract $3xy^2$

$$
\begin{array}{r}
13 \\
3 \\
\hline
10
\end{array}
$$

Now, subtract x^3

$$
\begin{array}{r}
1 \\
-1 \\
\hline
0
\end{array}
$$

Hence, required cube root $= 119$.

Chapter Practice

Exercise 1

1. Find the cube of the following.
   - (i) 18
   - (ii) 35
   - (iii) 78
   - (iv) 172
   - (v) 118
   - (vi) 1025
   - (vii) 109
   - (viii) 997
   - (ix) 999996
   - (x) 9995

2. Find the cube root of the following.
   - (i) 13824
   - (ii) 1601613
   - (iii) 1124864
   - (iv) 884736
   - (v) 92959677
   - (vi) 973242271
   - (vii) 830584
   - (viii) 250047
   - (ix) 1685159
   - (x) 1404928

Exercise 2

1. $(13)^3 - (13)^2$ is equal to   (OBC Clerk, 09)
   - (a) 73
   - (b) 2028
   - (c) 169
   - (d) 39

2. $1152 \div 36 + 9^3$ is equal to   (OBC Clerk, 09)
   - (a) 749
   - (b) 7231
   - (c) 738
   - (d) 761

3. If $(14)^3$ is added to the square of a number, then answer so obtained is 4425. What is the number ?   (OBC Clerk, 09)
   - (a) 1849
   - (b) 43
   - (c) 41
   - (d) 1681

4. $45^3 \times 11^2 - 3320^2$ is equal to   (Central Bank Clerk, 09)
   - (a) 3755
   - (b) 3745
   - (c) 3735
   - (d) 3725

5. If $(20)^3$ is subtracted from the square of a number, the answer so obtained is 4321. What is the number ?   (Central Bank Clerk, 09)
   - (a) 110
   - (b) 111
   - (c) 112
   - (d) 113

6. $36^3 \times 5^3 - 2400^2$ is equal to   (Indian Overseas Bank Clerk, 09)
   - (a) 720
   - (b) 720000
   - (c) 7200
   - (d) 72000

7. If $\sqrt[3]{13824} \times \sqrt{x} = 864$, then x is equal to   (SBI Clerk, 09)
   - (a) 1296
   - (b) 1156
   - (c) 1600
   - (d) 1024

8. If $\sqrt[3]{x} = (756 \times 67) \div 804$, then x is equal to (Nabard Bank Officer, 09)
   - (a) 195112
   - (b) 250047
   - (c) 226981
   - (d) 27462

9. $\sqrt[3]{4096}$ is equal to   (UCO Bank PO, 09)
   - (a) 16
   - (b) 26
   - (c) 18
   - (d) 24

10. $\sqrt[3]{1092727}$ is equal to (PNB PO, 09)
    (a) 108   (b) 103
    (c) 97   (d) 107

11. Cube root of 658503 is (MAT, 00)
    (a) 83   (b) 77
    (c) 87   (d) 97

12. The least possible value of A, for which $90 \times A$ is a perfect cube, is (CPO, 03)
    (a) 200   (b) 300
    (c) 500   (d) 600

13. By what number should 1497375 be multiplied to make it a perfect cube ?
    (a) 3   (b) 5   (Hotel Management, 01)
    (c) 9   (d) None of these

14. Sum of digits of the smallest number by which 1440 be multiplied so that it becomes a perfect cube is (SSC (GL), 03)
    (a) 4   (b) 6
    (c) 7   (d) 8

15. $\dfrac{\sqrt[3]{8}}{\sqrt{16}} \div \sqrt{\dfrac{100}{49}} \times \sqrt[3]{125}$ is equal to (SSC (GL), 99)

    (a) 7   (b) $1\dfrac{3}{4}$

    (c) $\dfrac{7}{100}$ (d) $\dfrac{4}{7}$

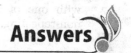

Answers

Exercise 1

1.   (i) 5832   (ii) 42875
   (iii) 474552   (iv) 5088448
    (v) 1643032   (vi) 1076890625
  (vii) 1295029   (viii) 991026973
   (ix) 999988000047999936   (x) 998500749875

2.   (i) 24   (ii) 117
   (iii) 104   (iv) 96
    (v) 453   (vi) 991
  (vii) 94   (viii) 63
   (ix) 119   (x) 112

Exercise 2

1. (b)   **2.** (d)   **3.** (c)   **4.** (d)   **5.** (b)
6. (d)   **7.** (a)   **8.** (b)   **9.** (a)   **10.** (b)
11. (c)   **12.** (b)   **13.** (a)   **14.** (b)   **15.** (b)

8 Decimals

Here, nothing is new about decimals but we will used methods to solve or simplify decimals as discussed in last chapters. First we know some important points about decimals.

(i) If the denominator of a fraction contains only 2 or 5 as factors, then fraction is non-repeating decimals.

eg, $\dfrac{1}{16} = \dfrac{1}{2^4} = 0.0625$ and $\dfrac{1}{50} = \dfrac{1}{5^2 \times 2} = 0.02$

(ii) If the denominator of a fraction contains 3, 7, 11, ... etc prime numbers except 2 and 5, then fraction is repeating decimals. eg,

$$\dfrac{1}{3} = 0.333\ldots = 0.\overline{3}$$

(iii) If the denominator of a fraction contains 3, 7, 11, ... etc prime numbers with one of either 2 or 5, then fraction is partly repeating or partly non-repeating.

Operations on Decimals

Conversion into Decimals

(i) If denominators of fraction are 9, 99, ... etc, then

$$\dfrac{1}{9} = 0.11111\ldots = 0.\overline{1} \quad \text{and} \quad \dfrac{1}{99} = 0.010101\ldots = 0.\overline{01} \text{ etc.}$$

(ii) If denominators of fraction are 3, 33, ... etc, then

$$\dfrac{1}{3} = 0.333\ldots = 0.\overline{3}$$

and $\dfrac{1}{33} = 0.0303\ldots = 0.\overline{03}$ etc.

(iii) A fraction can be represented as decimal using positive osculators.

    (a) First find the positive osculator and decide the last digit of the repeating block. Which is much clear with the following table.

Number	Positive osculator	Last digit of repeating block
19	2	1
29	3	1
13	4	3
23	7	3
7	5	7
and many more		

Positive osculator can be found as

make unit's place digit 9 and remaining portion is added to 1 and that resultant is positive osculator.

eg   ∵ . $41 \times 9 = 369$

∴   *Positive osculator for* $41 = 36 + 1 = 37$

and ∵ $13 \times 3 = 39$

∴   *Positive osculator for* $13 = 3 + 1 = 4$.

(b) Multiply the last digit of repeating block by positive osculator and continue the process till zero is obtained.

eg, For 1/19, osculator is 2 and last digit of repeating block is 9.

∴
$$\frac{1}{19} = {}_1 0\,5\,{}_1 2 6 3\,{}_1 1\,{}_1 5\,{}_1 7\,{}_1 8 9\,{}_1 4 7\,{}_1 3\,{}_1 6 8 4 2\,1$$

$$= 0.\overline{052631578947368421}$$

Now, for 1/39, positive osculator is 4 and last digit of repeating block is 1.

∴
$$\frac{1}{39} = {}_1 0_2\,2_2 5_1 6 4\,1 = 0.\overline{025641}$$

Now, to much clear take new 1/13 for which positive osculator is 4 and last digit of repeating block is 3.

∴
$$\frac{1}{13} = {}_3 0_2 7_3 6 9\,{}_1 2\,3 = 0.\overline{076923}$$

Addition of Decimals

To add some decimals first remove decimal points and put the power of 10 in denominator according to the position of decimal. Now, add them using vedic sutra discussed in the chapter "Addition".

Or

First make number of digits same in all decimals and add them without thinking about decimal and put that after addition.

Example 1 *Add* 3.125, 7.03, 8.005, 1.2376.

Solution $3.125 = \dfrac{3125}{1000} = \dfrac{31250}{10000}$

$7.03 = \dfrac{703}{100} = \dfrac{70300}{10000}$

$8.005 = \dfrac{8005}{1000} = \dfrac{80050}{10000}$

and $1.2376 = \dfrac{12376}{10000}$

Now, $3.125 + 7.03 + 8.005 + 1.2376$

$$= \frac{31250 + 70300 + 80050 + 12376}{10000}$$

$$= \frac{193976}{10000}$$

$$= 19.3976$$

Subtraction of Decimals

This method is same as discussed above.

Example 2 *Subtract* 7.32 *from* 8.1357.

Solution $\because$

$$7.32 = \frac{732}{100} = \frac{73200}{10000}$$

and

$$8.1357 = \frac{81357}{10000}$$

Now,

$$8.1357 - 7.32 = \frac{81357 - 73200}{10000}$$

$$= \frac{8157}{10000} = 0.8157$$

Multiplication of Decimals

First change decimals into fractions and then corresponding numerators and denominators are multiplied.

Example 3 *Multiply* 3.5 *and* 0.67.

Solution $\because$

$$3.5 = \frac{35}{10}$$

and

$$0.67 = \frac{67}{100}$$

$\therefore$

$$3.5 \times 0.67 = \frac{35}{10} \times \frac{67}{100} = \frac{2345}{1000} = 2.345$$

Division of Decimals

Division of decimals are discussed in the chapter "Division".

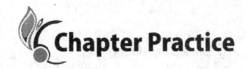

Chapter Practice

Exercise 1

1. Add the following
   (i) 31.94, 413.867, 2.891
   (ii) 3.098, 2.435
2. Subtract the first number from second
   (i) 43.81, 56.3
   (ii) 467.2435, 493.867
3. Multiply the following
   (i) 43.81 and 3.09
   (ii) 3.201 and 1.123
4. Solve
   (i) 249 ÷ 137   (ii) 367 ÷ 3.146 (upto three places of decimals)

Exercise 2

1. $(16 \times 36 \div 15 + 11)$ is equal to   (OBC Clerk, 09)
   (a) 43
   (b) 41.5
   (c) 47
   (d) 49.4

2. $(38.7 \times 14.5 \times 6.4)$ is equal to   (Central Bank Clerk, 09)
   (a) 3564.88
   (b) 3548.42
   (c) 3591.36
   (d) None of these

3. $(6.8 \times 8.8 \times 11.9 - 202.596)$ is equal to   (Central Bank Clerk, 09)
   (a) 510.5
   (b) 509.5
   (c) 508.5
   (d) 507.5

4. $(556.65 + 65.65 + 56.65)$ is equal to   (Central Bank Clerk, 09)
   (a) 676.05
   (b) 678.95
   (c) 682.55
   (d) 684.85

5. If $16.4 \times x = 590.4$, then x is equal to   (Central Bank Clerk, 09)
   (a) 31
   (b) 36
   (c) 35
   (d) 37

6. $(1276.34 - 783.11 + 217.84)$ is equal to   (Central Bank Clerk, 09)
   (a) 691.07
   (b) 711.07
   (c) 701.07
   (d) 681.07

7. If $9.3 \times x = 523.59$, then x is equal to   (Indian Overseas Bank Clerk, 09)
   (a) 56.3
   (b) 68.9
   (c) 42.7
   (d) 74.8

8. $(43.34 + 44.33 + 343.43)$ is equal to   (Indian Overseas Bank Clerk, 09)
   (a) 456.01
   (b) 431.1
   (c) 444.33
   (d) 428.9

9. $(68.8 \times 14.7 \times 7.1)$ is equal to   (Indian Overseas Bank Clerk, 09)
   (a) 7108.565
   (b) 7018.665
   (c) 7180.656
   (d) 7081.556

10. $(3.7 \times 8.2 \times 10.8 - 29.921)$ is equal to   (Indian Overseas Bank Clerk, 09)
    (a) 287.951   (b) 307.951   (c) 297.751   (d) 317.951

11. (2.5×1.5) is equal to   (Dena Bank Clerk, 09)
    (a) 37.5   (b) 3.75   (c) 0.375   (d) 22.5

12. If $15.75 \div 2.25 = 0.7 \times x$, then x is equal to   (Dena Bank Clerk, 09)
    (a) 7   (b) 10   (c) 0.07   (d) 1

13. $(3.5 + 11.25 \times 4.5 - 32.5)$ is equal to   (SBI Clerk, 09)
    (a) 18.275   (b) 21.625   (c) 32.375   (d) 25.45

14. $(15.593 - 9.214 - 3.452 - 2.191)$ is equal to   (Dena Bank PO, 09)
    (a) 1.874   (b) 0.686   (c) 2.342   (d) 0.736

15. $(666.66 + 66.66 + 6.66 + 6 + 0.66)$ is equal to   (Dena Bank PO, 09)
    (a) 746.64   (b) 764.64   (c) 766.64   (d) 744.64

16. $(0.3 + 3 + 3.33 + 3.3 + 3.03 + 333)$ is equal to   (Nabard Bank Officer, 09)
    (a) 375.66   (b) 345.99   (c) 375.93   (d) None of these

17. $(34.12)^2 - \sqrt{7396}$ is equal to   (Nabard Bank Officer, 09)
    (a) 1080.1744   (b) 1078.1474   (c) 1078.1744   (d) 1080.1474

18. $(21.35)^2 + (12.25)^2$ is equal to   (PNB PO, 09)
    (a) 171.4125   (b) 605.885   (c) 604.085   (d) 463.1825

19. $(334.41 + 47.26 + 1.25 + 5 + 0.66)$ is equal to   (PNB PO, 09)
    (a) 411.24   (b) 396.15   (c) 388.58   (d) 376.85

20. The value of $\sqrt[3]{\sqrt{0.000064}}$ is   (MAT, 99)
    (a) 0.02   (b) 0.2   (c) 2.0   (d) None of these

Answers

Exercise 1

1. (i) 448.698   (ii) 5.533   **2.** (i) 12.49   (ii) 26.6235
3. (i) 135.3729   (ii) 3.594723   **4.** (i) 1.817   (ii) 116.656

Exercise 2

1. (d)	**2.** (c)	**3.** (b)	**4.** (b)	**5.** (b)
6. (b)	**7.** (a)	**8.** (b)	**9.** (c)	**10.** (c)
11. (b)	**12.** (b)	**13.** (b)	**14.** (d)	**15.** (a)
16. (d)	**17.** (c)	**18.** (b)	**19.** (c)	**20.** (b)

9   Factorization

Factorization is a process of spliting a polynomial into the product of two or more polynomials. This is an important process to find the value of any variable. But its conventional method is very complicated, so we use vedic sutra to factorize the quadratic and cubic polynomials. Vedic sutra "Anurupyena" and "Adyamadye Nant yamantyena" are used which means "Proportionately" and "The first by the first and the last by the last" respectively. We classified polynomials in four category to factorization method:

   (i) Simple quadratic polynomials
   (ii) Homogeneous quadratic polynomials
  (iii) Complex quadratic non-homogeneous polynomials
  (iv) Cubic polynomials

Simple Quadratic Polynomials

Let the simple quadratic polynomial is $ax^2 + bx + c$ which have to factorize.

The following steps should be follow.

Step I   Split b in two numbers p and q such that $b = p + q$ and $a : p :: q : c :: r : s$ (say)

                Thus, first factor will be $(rx + s)$.

Step II   Find $\dfrac{a}{r}$ and $\dfrac{c}{s}$, then other factor will be $\left(\dfrac{a}{r} x + \dfrac{c}{s}\right)$.

Example 1   *Factorize* $3x^2 + 14x + 8$.

Solution $\because$ $14 = 12 + 2$

$\Rightarrow$ $a : p = 3 : 12 = 1 : 4$

and $q : c = 2 : 8 = 1 : 4$

$\Rightarrow$ $a : p :: q : c :: 1 : 4$

Thus, first factor is $x + 4$.

Now, second factor is $\left(\dfrac{3}{1} x + \dfrac{8}{4}\right)$ *ie,* $(3x + 2)$

Hence, $3x^2 + 14x + 8 = (3x + 2)(x + 4)$

Example 2   *Factorize* $8x^2 - 70x - 18$.

Solution $\because$ $-70 = -72 + 2$

                 $a : p = 8 : (-72) = 1 : (-9)$

and
$$q:c = 2:(-18) = 1:(-9)$$
$$\Rightarrow \qquad a:p::q:c::1:(-9)$$

Thus, first factor is $(x-9)$.

Now, second factor is $\left(\dfrac{8}{1}x - \dfrac{18}{(-9)}\right) = (8x+2)$

Hence, $\qquad 8x^2 - 70x - 18 = (8x+2)(x-9)$

Homogeneous Quadratic Polynomials

Let the general homogeneous quadratic polynomial is $ax^2 + hxy + by^2 = 0$.

Procedure is same as case (i) but should be remember about variables. Only following steps have to follow.

Step I Split h in two factors p and q such that $a:p::q:b::r:s$ and $h = p+q$

Thus, first factor will be $(rx + sy)$.

Find $\dfrac{a}{r}$ and $\dfrac{b}{s}$. Thus, another factor will be $\left(\dfrac{a}{r}x + \dfrac{b}{s}y\right)$.

Example 3 *Factorize* $4x^2 + 15xy + 9y^2$.

Solution $\because$ $\qquad\qquad 15 = 12 + 3$

$\Rightarrow \qquad\qquad a:p = 4:12 = 1:3$

and $\qquad\qquad q:b = 3:9 = 1:3$

$\Rightarrow \qquad\qquad a:p::q:b::1:3$.

Thus, first factor is $(x + 3y)$ and second factor is $\left(\dfrac{4}{1}x + \dfrac{9}{3}y\right)$ ie, $(4x + 3y)$.

Hence, $\qquad 4x^2 + 15xy + 9y^2 = (x+3y)(4x+3y)$

To factorize any homogeneous equation of more than two variables, we use vedic sutra "Lopanasthapanabhyam" which means "by alternate elimination and retention first" and further process is clear in the following example.

Example 4 *Factorize* $6x^2 + 5y^2 + 8z^2 + 13xy + 16xz + 14yz$.

Solution Put $z = 0$ to get the expression as
$$6x^2 + 13xy + 5y^2$$

$\because \qquad\qquad 13 = 10 + 3$

$\therefore \qquad\qquad a:p = 6:10 = 3:5$

and $\qquad\qquad q:b = 3:5$

Thus, first factor is $(3x + 5y)$ and other factor is $\left(\dfrac{6}{3}x + \dfrac{5}{5}y\right)$ ie, $(2x + y)$.

Now, put $y = 0$, to get the expression as
$$6x^2 + 16xz + 8z^2$$

Now, $\qquad 6:12::4:8::1:2$ ie, $(2x + 4z)$

Thus, first factor is $(x + 2z)$ and other factor is $\left(\dfrac{6}{2}x + \dfrac{8}{4}z\right)$ ie, $(3x + 2z)$

From the factors it is clear that
$$6x^2 + 5y^2 + 8z^2 + 13xy + 16xz + 14yz$$
$$= (2x + y + 4z)(3x + 5y + 2z)$$

Complex Quadratic Non-Homogeneous Polynomials

If polynomials are non-homogeneous quadratic polynomials, then the procedure is different. To factorize the vedic sutra "Lopanasthapanabhyam" is used and process is discussed in the following example.

Example 5   *Factorize* $2x^2 - 15y^2 - xy + x + 41y - 28$.

Solution   Put $y = 0$ to get the expression
$$2x^2 + x - 28.$$
Since, the factors of this expression are $(x + 4)$ and $(2x - 7)$.
Now, put $x = 0$, to get the expression.
$$-15y^2 + 41y - 28.$$
Since, the factors of this expression are $(-3y + 4)$ and $(5y - 7)$.
Thus, $2x^2 - 15y^2 - xy + x + 41y - 28$
$$= (x - 3y + 4)(2x + 5y - 7).$$

Cubic Polynomials

To factorize a cubic polynomial first find one linear factor by applying remainder theorem or by simple observation. To find the other two factors first we have to find a quadratic polynomial where first and last term is find using vedic sutra "Adyamadyena" and to find middle term "Gunitasamuchchaya" is used. The following steps should be followed to factorize a cubic polynomial.

Step I   Find the one linear factor using remainder theorem or by simple observation.

Step II   For quadratic polynomial, first and last term of the quadratic polynomial are choosed from given cubic polynomial and middle term is determined using vedic sutra "Gunitasamuchchaya".
Coefficient of middle term
$$= \left\{ \frac{\text{Sum of coefficient of different terms in cubic}}{\text{Sum of coefficients of the terms of first factor}} \right\} - \left\{ \begin{array}{l} \text{Sum of coefficients of} \\ \text{first and last terms of} \\ \text{quadratic obtained above} \end{array} \right\}$$

This method is much clear with help of the following example.

Example 6   *Factorize* $x^3 + 10x^2 + 31x + 30$.

Solution   Using remainder theorem.
at $x = -2$
$$(-2)^3 + 10(-2)^2 + 31(-2) + 30$$
$$= -8 + 40 - 62 + 30 = 0$$

Since, given polynomial is zero at $x = -2$.

Therefore, $x + 2$ is one factor.

Let first and last term of quadratic polynomial are 1 and 15.

Now, coefficients of middle term

$$= \frac{(1 + 10 + 31 + 30)}{(1 + 2)} - (1 + 15)$$

$$= 24 - 16 = 8.$$

∴ Quadratic polynomial is $x^2 + 8x + 15$ whose factors using method of factoring quadratic polynomials are $(x + 3)$ and $(x + 5)$

Hence, $x^3 + 10x^2 + 31x + 30 = (x + 2)(x + 3)(x + 5)$

(1) *If $(x + a)(x + b)(x + c) = x^3 + (a + b + c)\, x^2 + (ab + bc + ca)x + abc$.*

(2) *These factors can be verified using vedic sutra "Gunitasamuchchaya Samuchchayagunita", whose meaning and uses have been discussed in list of sutra.*

Chapter Practice

Exercise 1

1. Factorize the following quadratic polynomials.

(i) $8x^2 - 70x - 18$

(ii) $2x^2 - 5x - 3$

(iii) $3x^2 - 7x + 2$

(iv) $6x^2 + 37x + 6$

(v) $9x^2 - 15x + 4$

(vi) $12x^2 - 23xy + 10y^2$

(vii) $6x^2 - 14xy + 4y^2$

(viii) $3x^2 + y^2 + 9z^2 + 4xy + 6yz + 12xz$

(ix) $2x^2 - 15y^2 - xy + x + 41y - 28$

(x) $4x^2 - 7y^2 - 9z^2 + 12xy - 16xz + 16yz$

2. Factorize the following cubic polynomials.

(i) $x^3 + 6x^2 + 11x + 6$

(ii) $x^3 + 12x^2 + 44x + 48$

(iii) $x^3 + 3x^2 - 17x - 38$

(iv) $x^3 - 7x + 6$

(v) $x^3 - 2x^2 - 23x + 60$

Exercise 2

1. Factors of $4x^2 - 12x + 9$ are

(a) $(2x - 3)(2x + 3)$

(b) $(2x - 3)(2x - 3)$

(c) $(2x + 3)(2x + 3)$

(d) None of these

2. Factors of $6x^2 + x - 12$ are

(a) $(2x + 3)(3x - 4)$

(b) $(2x + 3)(3x + 4)$

(c) $(2x - 3)(3x + 4)$

(d) $(2x - 3)(3x - 4)$

3. Factors of $4x^2 - 9x - 100$ are

(a) $(4x - 25)(x + 4)$

(b) $(x + 4)(4x + 25)$

(c) $(x - 4)(4x + 25)$

(d) None of these

4. Factors of $x^2 - x + 2$ are

(a) $(x + 7)(x + 2)(x - 7)$

(b) $\left(x - \dfrac{1 + \sqrt{-7}}{2}\right)\left(x + \dfrac{1 - \sqrt{-7}}{2}\right)$

(c) $(x + 7)(x + 3)$

(d) None of these

5. Factors of $x^2 - 18x + 77$ are

(a) $(x - 11)(x + 7)$

(b) $(x + 11)(x + 7)$

(c) $(x - 11)(x - 7)$

(d) None of these

6. Factors of $15x^2 - 28y^2 - xy$ are

(a) $(5x - 7y)(3x - 4y)$

(b) $(5x + 7y)(4x - 3y)$

(c) $(5x + 7y)(3x + 4y)$

(d) $(5x + 7y)(3x - 4y)$

7. Factors of $4y^2 - 11xy - 3x^2$ are

(a) $(y - 3x)(y - x)$

(b) $(y - 3x)(4y + x)$

(c) $(y + 3x)(4y + x)$

(d) None of these

8. Factors of $a^3 + a^2 + 2a + 8$ are

(a) $(a + 2)(a^2 - a + 4)$

(b) $(a - 2)(a^2 - a - 4)$

(c) $(a + 2)(a^2 - 2a + 1)$

(d) $(a + 2)(a - 1)(a + 4)$

9. Factors of $2x^3 + 19x^2 + 38x + 21$ are

    (a) $(2x + 3)(x + 5)(x + 1)$ (b) $(4x + 9)(2x + 1)(x + 1)$

    (c) $(x + 1)(x + 4)(2x + 1)$ (d) $(x + 1)(x + 7)(2x + 3)$

10. Factors of $(x^2 + 2x)^2 - 3(x^2 + 2x) - y(x^2 + 2x) + 3y$ are

    (a) $(x^2 + 2x - 3)(x^2 - 2x - 1)$ (b) $(x^2 + 2x - 3)(x^2 - 2x + y)$

    (c) $(x^2 + 2x - 3)(x^2 + 2x - y)$ (d) $(x^2 + 2x - 3)(x^2 - 2x - y)$

Answers

Exercise 1

1.   (i) $(8x + 2)(x - 9)$ (ii) $(x - 3)(2x + 1)$

       (iii) $(x - 2)(3x - 1)$ (iv) $(x + 6)(6x + 1)$

        (v) $(3x - 1)(3x - 4)$ (vi) $(3x - 2y)(4x - 5y)$

      (vii) $(x - 2y)(6x - 2y)$ (viii) $(x + y + 3z)(3x + y + 3z)$

       (ix) $(2x + 7y - 9z)(2x - y + z)$ (x) $(x - 3y + 4)(2x + 5y - 7)$

2.   (i) $(x + 1)(x + 2)(x + 3)$ (ii) $(x + 2)(x + 4)(x + 6)$

       (iii) $(x + 2)(x^2 + x - 19)$ (iv) $(x - 1)(x - 2)(x + 3)$

        (v) $(x - 3)(x - 4)(x + 5)$

Exercise 2

1. (b)	**2.** (a)	**3.** (a)	**4.** (b)	**5.** (c)
6. (d)	**7.** (b)	**8.** (a)	**9.** (d)	**10.** (c)

10 Highest Common Factor (HCF)

Highest Common Factor (HCF) is also known as Greatest Common Divisor (GCD). As usual in comparison to its conventional method vedic method is easy to use. Vedic sutra "Loponasthapanabhyam", Sankalan Vyavakalam" and "Adyam-Adyena" are used.

To find HCF following step have to follow **using subtraction method.**

Step I   Let $P(x)$ and $Q(x)$ be two polynomials, first make the coefficient of maximum power of variable same in both polynomials.

Step II   Subtract second polynomial from first polynomial.

Step III   Take common any term which is in each term.

Step IV   Resultant linear or quadratic polynomial is required HCF.

Now, to find HCF **using addition method** following steps have to follow.

Step I   Let two polynomials $P(x)$ and $Q(x)$ be two polynomials, first make constant term same.

Step II   Now, add $P(x)$ and $Q(x)$. Take anything is common in each term.

Step III   Resultant linear or quadratic polynomial is required HCF.

Example 1   Find the HCF of $x^2 + x - 42$ and $x^2 + 18x + 77$.

Solution   Since coefficient of maximum power of x are same.

Let $P(x) = x^2 + x - 42$

and $Q(x) = x^2 + 18x + 77$

Now, $P(x) - Q(x) = (x^2 + x - 42) - (x^2 + 18x + 77)$
$$= x - 42 - 18x - 77 = -17x - 119 = -17(x + 7)$$

Hence, required HCF $= x + 7$

Example 2   Find the HCF of $x^3 + 2x^2 + 4x + 3$ and $x^3 + 2x^2 - 1$.

Solution   Let $P(x) = x^3 + 2x^2 + 4x + 3$

and $Q(x) = x^3 + 2x^2 - 1 = 3x^3 + 6x^2 - 3$

Now, constant terms in $P(x)$ and $Q(x)$ are same.

$\therefore$ $P(x) + Q(x) = (x^3 + 2x^2 + 4x + 3) + (3x^3 + 6x^2 - 3)$
$$= x^3 + 2x^2 + 4x + 3 + 3x^3 + 6x^2 - 3 = 4x^3 + 8x^2 + 4x$$
$$= 4x(x^2 + 2x + 1) = 4x(x + 1)^2$$

Hence, required HCF $= (x + 1)^2$

Chapter Practice

Exercise 1

Find the HCF of the following.

1. $x^2 - 3x - 108, x^2 - 29x + 204$

2. $x^2 - 5x - 6, x^2 + 7x + 6$

3. $x^3 - 3x^2 - 4x + 12, x^3 - 7x^2 + 16x - 12$

4. $4x^3 + 13x^2 + 19x + 4, 2x^3 + 5x^2 + 5x - 4$

5. $6x^4 - 7x^3 - 5x^2 + 14x + 7, 6x^4 - 10x^3 + 14x$

6. $2x^3 + x^2 - 9, x^4 + 2x^2 + 9$

7. $x^3 + 3x^2 - 5x - 4, x^5 - x^4 - x^3 - 4x^2 + 4x + 4$

8. $x^6 - 1, x^6 - x^5 - x^4 - 2x^3 + x^2 + x + 1$

9. $x^3 + 2x^2 + 4x + 3, x^3 + 2x^2 - 1$

10. $x^3 - 5x^2 - 13x - 7, x^2 + 2x + 1$

Exercise 2

1. HCF of $x^3 - 1$ and $x^4 + x^2 + 1$ is
   (a) $x - 1$ (b) $x^2 + 1$ (c) $x^2 + x + 1$ (d) $x^2 - x + 1$

2. HCF of $2x^4 + 243x$ and $24x^3 - 54x$ is
   (a) $x(2x + 3)$ (b) $2x(2x + 3)$ (c) $4x(x + 3)$ (d) $(x + 54)$

3. HCF of $x^4 + 3x^2 - 4$ and $x^4 - 4x^2 + 3$ is
   (a) $x - 1$ (b) $x + 1$ (c) $x^2 - 1$ (d) $x^2 - 3$

4. HCF of $2(a^2 - b^2)$ and $3(a^3 - b^3)$ is
   (a) $a + b$ (b) $a - b$
   (c) $2(a - b)$ (d) None of these

5. HCF of $p^2 - p - 6$ and $p^2 - 3p - 18$ is
   (a) $p - 6$ (b) $p + 3$ (c) $p + 2$ (d) $p - 2$

Answers

Exercise 1

1. $x - 12$ 2. $x + 1$ 3. $x^2 - 5x + 6$ 4. $x^2 + 3x + 4$
5. $3x^3 - 5x^2 + 7$ 6. $x^2 + 2x + 3$ 7. $x^2 - x - 1$ 8. $x^3 - 1$
9. $x + 1$ 10. $x^2 + 2x + 1$

Exercise 2

1. (c) 2. (d) 3. (c) 4. (b) 5. (a)

11 Simple Equations

The equations in one variable or equations which are not complicated, are called simple equations. To solve these simple equations vedic sutra "Paravartya Yojayet" is widely used which means "transpose and adjust".

The types of simple equations are as follows

Type I   Let the equation is

$$px + q = rx + s$$
$$\Rightarrow \qquad px - rx = s - q$$
$$\Rightarrow \qquad (p - r)\, x = s - q$$
$$\Rightarrow \qquad x = \frac{s - q}{p - r}$$

Example 1   *Solve* $2x + 7 = x + 9$

Solution   Here $p = 2, q = 7, r = 1, s = 9$

$$\therefore \qquad x = \frac{9 - 7}{2 - 1}$$
$$= \frac{2}{1} = 2$$

Type II   If the equation is $(x + p)\,(x + q) = (x + r)\,(x + s)$

If $\qquad p \times q = r \times s$, then $x = 0$

if $\qquad p \times q \neq r \times s$, then $x = \dfrac{rs - pq}{p + q - r - s}$

Example 2   *Solve for x,* $(x + 7)\,(x + 9) = (x + 3)\,(x + 21).$

Solution   Here $p = 7, q = 9, r = 3, s = 21$

Since, $\qquad p \times q = 7 \times 9 = 63$

and $\qquad r \times s = 3 \times 21 = 63$

$\Rightarrow \qquad p \times q = r \times s$

$\therefore \qquad x = 0$

Type III   Let the equation is

$$\frac{px + q}{rx + s} = \frac{t}{u}$$

$$\therefore \qquad u\,(px + q) = t\,(rx + s)$$

$$\Rightarrow \qquad upx + uq = trx + ts$$
$$\Rightarrow \qquad x\,(up - tr) = ts - uq$$
$$\Rightarrow \qquad x = \frac{ts - uq}{up - tr}$$

Example 3 *Solve for* x, $\dfrac{5 - 6x}{3x - 1} = \dfrac{1}{2}$

Solution   Since, $p = -1, q = 5, r = 3, s = -1, t = 1$ and $u = 2$

$$\therefore \qquad x = \frac{-1 \times 1 - 2 \times 5}{2 \times (-1) - (1)(3)}$$

$$= \frac{-1 - 10}{-2 - 3}$$

$$= \frac{-11}{-5}$$

$$= \frac{11}{5}$$

Type IV   Let the equation be

$$\frac{a}{x + p} + \frac{b}{x + q} = 0$$

$$\Rightarrow \qquad a\,(x + q) + b\,(x + p) = 0$$
$$\Rightarrow \qquad ax + aq + bx + bp = 0$$
$$\Rightarrow \qquad (a + b)\,x = -(aq + bp)$$
$$\Rightarrow \qquad x = -\left(\frac{aq + bp}{a + b}\right)$$

Example 4   *Let the equation is* $\dfrac{1}{x - 1} + \dfrac{4}{x + 5} = 0$. Find the value of x.

Solution   Here $a = 1, b = 4, p = -1, q = 5$

$$\therefore \qquad x = -\left(\frac{1 \times 5 - 4 \times 1}{1 + 4}\right)$$

$$= -\frac{1}{5}$$

If $\dfrac{a}{x + b} + \dfrac{a}{x + c} = 0$, then $(x + b) + (x + c) = 0$

Type V   Let the equation be $ax + bx = cx + dx$,

then using vedic sutra "Sunyam samyasamuchchaya" is used which means "when the samuchchaya is same that samuchchaya is zero".

Thus, $x = 0$

Type VI   Let the equation be

$$\frac{ax + b}{cx + d} = \frac{cx + d}{ax + b}$$

Thus, $(ax + b) + (cx + d) = 0$

$\Rightarrow$ $(a + c)\,x = -(b + d)$

$\Rightarrow$ $x = -\left(\dfrac{b + d}{a + c}\right)$

Example 5   *Solve for x,* $\dfrac{2x - 3}{7x - 6} = \dfrac{7x - 6}{2x - 3}$

Solution   Here the form is as

$\dfrac{ax + b}{cx + d} = \dfrac{cx + d}{ax + b}$, then $(ax + b) + (cx + d) = 0$

$\therefore$ $2x - 3 + 7x - 6 = 0$

$\Rightarrow$ $9x = 9$

$\Rightarrow$ $x = 1$

Some cases are also there which can be reduces to last six types, first change to the proper form and apply corresponding method.

Chapter Practice

Exercise 1

Solve for x.

1. $9x + 9 = 7x + 7$

2. $\dfrac{1}{2x - 1} + \dfrac{1}{3x - 1} = 0$

3. $\dfrac{2x + 9}{2x + 7} = \dfrac{2x + 7}{2x + 9}$

4. $\dfrac{3x + 4}{6x + 7} = \dfrac{5x + 6}{2x + 3}$

5. $\dfrac{1}{x - 7} + \dfrac{1}{x - 9} = \dfrac{1}{x - 6} + \dfrac{1}{x - 10}$

6. $\dfrac{x - 2}{x - 3} + \dfrac{x - 3}{x - 4} = \dfrac{x - 1}{x - 2} + \dfrac{x - 4}{x - 5}$

7. $\dfrac{3}{x + 1} + \dfrac{4}{x + 2} = \dfrac{7}{x + 3}$

8. $\dfrac{1}{x + 2} + \dfrac{3}{x + 3} + \dfrac{5}{x + 5} = \dfrac{9}{x + 4}$

9. $\dfrac{7}{x + 6} + \dfrac{1}{x + 2} + \dfrac{10}{x + 1} = \dfrac{18}{x + 3}$

10. $\dfrac{2x + 7}{3x + 10} = \dfrac{6x + 19}{x + 3}$

Exercise 2

1. If $25x - 19 - \{3 - (4x - 5)\} = 3x - (6x - 5)$, then x is equal to
   (a) 7
   (b) −1
   (c) 2
   (d) 3

2. If $\dfrac{3x + 6}{8} - \dfrac{11x - 8}{24} + \dfrac{x}{3} = \dfrac{3x}{4} + \dfrac{x + 7}{24}$, then x is equal to
   (a) −3
   (b) $\dfrac{19}{13}$
   (c) 2
   (d) 4

3. If $(x + 7)(x + 9) = (x + 3)(x + 21)$, then x is equal to
   (a) 0
   (b) 1
   (c) 2
   (d) 3

4. If $\dfrac{5 - 6x}{3x - 1} = \dfrac{1}{2}$, then x is equal to
   (a) $\dfrac{11}{15}$
   (b) 0
   (c) $\dfrac{1}{2}$
   (d) $-\dfrac{11}{15}$

5. If $\dfrac{1}{x - 7} + \dfrac{1}{x - 9} = \dfrac{1}{x - 6} + \dfrac{1}{x - 10}$, then x is equal to
   (a) 1
   (b) 7
   (c) 8
   (d) 10

6. If $\dfrac{1}{2x - 1} + \dfrac{1}{3x - 1} = 0$, then x is equal to
   (a) $\dfrac{2}{5}$
   (b) $\dfrac{5}{2}$
   (c) $\dfrac{1}{2}$
   (d) 0

7. If $(x - 6)(x + 7) = (x + 3)(x - 11)$, then x is equal to
   (a) 1
   (b) 2
   (c) 0
   (d) None of these

8. If $\dfrac{1}{x + 2} + \dfrac{1}{x + 1} = 0$, then x is equal to
   (a) 0
   (b) $-\dfrac{3}{2}$
   (c) $\dfrac{3}{2}$
   (d) $\dfrac{1}{2}$

Answers

Exercise 1

1. -1

2. $\dfrac{2}{5}$

3. -4

4. $-\dfrac{5}{4}$

5. 8

6. $3\dfrac{1}{2}$

7. $-\dfrac{8}{5}$

8. $-2\dfrac{1}{2}$

9. $-\dfrac{51}{26}$

10. $-\dfrac{13}{4}$

Exercise 2

1. (a)

2. (b)

3. (a)

4. (a)

5. (c)

6. (a)

7. (a)

8. (b)

12 Quadratic Equations

As, the quadratics occur quite frequently in many problems of Science and Engineering, the mastry over their solution became unavoidable. As we know that the equation of the form $ax^2 + bx + c = 0$ is a quadratic equation, where a, b and c are constants.

For factorization of quadratic expressions, we use the following two sub sutras of Vedic Mathematics.

(i) Anurupyena

(ii) Adyamadye Nantyamantyena

Whose meaning are "Proportionately" and "the first by the first and the last by the last" respectively.

The procedure for the factorization is as follows

Step I   For splitting the middle term we use 'Anurupyena' *sutra*. Split the middle coefficient into two such parts that the ratio of the first coefficient to the first split part is the same as the ratio of the second split part to the last coefficient; *ie.*, $a/b_1 = b_2/c$. This ratio gives one of the two factors.

Step II   Obtain the second factor by dividing the first coefficient of the quadratic by the first coefficient of the first factor already found and the last coefficient of the quadratic by the last coefficient of that (first) factor. Here, we are using Adyamadye Nantyamantyena *sutra*.

Solving Quadratic Equations

The quadratic equation is of the form

$$ax^2 + bx + c = 0$$

We have already seen the method of factorization of quadratic expressions. For example,

$$2x^2 + 7x + 5 = (x + 1)(2x + 5)$$

If this expression is equated to zero, we readily get the solution in the form of two equations

$$(x + 1) = 0 \qquad \Rightarrow \quad x = -1$$
and $\quad (2x + 5) = 0 \qquad \Rightarrow \quad x = -2.5$

However, for some equations, there may not be such integer factors. For example

$$6x^2 + 5x - 3 = 0$$

For solving such quadratic equations quickly, we use the following Vedic Mathematics method.

Rule The first differential of a quadratic expression is equal to the square root of its discriminant. Representing the symbolically,

$$D_1 = \sqrt{\text{discriminant}} = \sqrt{b^2 - 4ac}$$

Thus,

$$D_1 = \frac{d}{dx}(6x^2 + 5x - 3)$$

$$= 12x + 5 = \sqrt{25 + 72} = \sqrt{97}$$

So, the first root is given by $\qquad 12x + 5 = \sqrt{97}$

and the second root is given by $\quad x + 5 = -\sqrt{97}$

This vedic method is very convenient and can be applied to any quadratic equation. But to solve other special type, some other vedic sutra is applied.

***Type* I** Let the equation be $\qquad x + \dfrac{1}{x} = \dfrac{d}{a}$

But by using vedic sutra "Vilokanam"

$$x + \frac{1}{x} = a + \frac{1}{a}$$

Thus, $\qquad\qquad\qquad x = a \text{ or } \dfrac{1}{a}$

Example 1 *Solve* $\dfrac{x}{x+4} + \dfrac{x+4}{x} = \dfrac{122}{11}$

Solution By vedic sutra "Vilokanam"

$$\frac{x}{x+4} + \frac{x+4}{x} = 11 + \frac{1}{11}$$

$$\Rightarrow \qquad\qquad \frac{x}{x+4} = 11$$

or $\qquad\qquad \dfrac{x}{x+4} = \dfrac{1}{11}$

$$\Rightarrow \qquad\qquad x = 11x + 44$$

or $\qquad\qquad 11x = x + 4$

$$\Rightarrow \qquad\qquad \frac{-44}{10} = x$$

or $\qquad\qquad x = \dfrac{4}{10}$

$$\Rightarrow \qquad\qquad x = -\frac{22}{5} \text{ or } \frac{2}{5}$$

***Type* II** Let the equation be

$$\frac{N_1}{D_1} = \frac{N_2}{D_2}$$

Now, if $\qquad\qquad N_1 + N_2 = D_1 + D_2$

Then, by vedic sutra "Shunyam Samuchchaya"

$$N_1 + N_2 = 0$$

and now,
$$N_1 - D_1 = (-1)(N_2 - D_2)$$

Thus,
$$N_1 - D_1 = 0$$

Example 2 *Solve the equation*

$$\frac{19x + 7}{12x - 11} = \frac{6x - 39}{13x - 21}$$

Solution Here, $N_1 = 19x + 7, N_2 = 6x - 39$

$$D_1 = 12x - 11 \text{ and } D_2 = 13x - 21$$

Now $N_1 + N_2 = 19x + 7 + 6x - 39 = 25x - 32$

and $D_1 + D_2 = 12x - 11 + 13x - 21 = 25x - 32$

$\Rightarrow$ $N_1 + N_2 = D_1 + D_2$

Thus, $25x - 32 = 0$

$\Rightarrow$ $x = \dfrac{32}{25}$

Now, $N_1 - D_1 = 19x + 7 - 12x + 11 = 7x + 18$

and $N_2 - D_2 = 6x - 39 - 13x + 21 = -7x - 18$

$$= -(7x + 18) = -(N_1 - D_1)$$

Thus, $7x + 18 = 0$

$$x = -\frac{18}{7}$$

Hence, both roots are $\dfrac{32}{25}$ and $\dfrac{-18}{7}$.

Type III Let the equation is of the form

$$\frac{l + n}{x + (l + n)} + \frac{m - n}{x + (m - n)} = \frac{l}{x + l} + \frac{m}{x + m}$$

In this case $N_1 + N_2 = N_3 + N_4$

Then, one root is zero *ie*, $x = 0$.

Also, another root, is calculated using

$$D_1 + D_2 = D_3 + D_4 = 0$$

· **Example 3** *Solve the equation* $\dfrac{4}{9x + 4} + \dfrac{5}{9x + 5} = \dfrac{1}{9x + 1} + \dfrac{8}{9x + 8}$

Solution Here, $N_1 + N_2 = 4 + 5 = 9$

and $N_3 + N_4 = 1 + 8 = 9$

$\Rightarrow$ $N_1 + N_2 = N_3 + N_4$

$\therefore$ $x = 0$

Now, $D_1 + D_2 = 9x + 4 + 9x + 5 = 18x + 9$

and $D_3 + D_4 = 9x + 1 + 9x + 8 = 18x + 9$

$\Rightarrow$ $D_1 + D_2 = D_3 + D_4$

Thus, for another root $18x + 9 = 0$

$\Rightarrow$ $x = -\dfrac{9}{18} = -\dfrac{1}{2}$

Chapter Practice

Exercise 1

Solve the following equations

1. $x + \dfrac{1}{x} = \dfrac{17}{4}$

2. $4x^2 - 4x + 1 = 0$

3. $\dfrac{5x+9}{5x-9} - \dfrac{5x-9}{5x+9} = \dfrac{56}{45}$

4. $\dfrac{3x+4}{6x+7} = \dfrac{5x+6}{2x+3}$

5. $\dfrac{2}{x+2} + \dfrac{3}{x+3} = \dfrac{4}{x+4} + \dfrac{1}{x+1}$

6. $\dfrac{2}{x+2} + \dfrac{3}{x+3} = \dfrac{5}{x+5}$

7. $\dfrac{6}{5x+6} + \dfrac{5}{6x+5} = \dfrac{2}{x+2} + \dfrac{1}{30x+1}$

8. $\dfrac{2}{x+2} + \dfrac{9}{x+9} = \dfrac{3}{x+3} + \dfrac{8}{x+8}$

9. $\dfrac{8}{x+4} + \dfrac{21}{x+7} = \dfrac{15}{x+3}$

10. $\dfrac{4x+3}{x+24} + \dfrac{7x+3}{x+12} = \dfrac{11x+3}{x+8}$

Exercise 2

1. If $6x^2 + 11x + 3 = 0$, then x is equal to

(a) $\dfrac{1}{3}, \dfrac{4}{3}$ (b) $\dfrac{-1}{3}, \dfrac{-3}{2}$ (c) $\dfrac{1}{3}, -3$ (d) None of these

2. If $48x^2 - 13x - 1 = 0$, then x is equal to

(a) $\dfrac{1}{3}, \dfrac{1}{16}$ (b) $\dfrac{1}{3}, \dfrac{-1}{16}$ (c) $\dfrac{1}{3}, 16$ (d) None of these

3. If $\dfrac{1}{x+4} + (x+4) = \dfrac{82}{9}$, then x is equal to

(a) $5, \dfrac{-35}{9}$ (b) $\dfrac{35}{9}, 5$ (c) $\dfrac{35}{9}, \dfrac{1}{5}$ (d) None of these

4. If $\dfrac{x}{x+4} + \dfrac{x+4}{x} = \dfrac{145}{12}$, then x is equal to

(a) $\dfrac{-48}{11}, \dfrac{1}{11}$ (b) $\dfrac{48}{11}, \dfrac{4}{11}$ (c) $\dfrac{-48}{11}, \dfrac{4}{11}$ (d) None of these

5. If $\dfrac{19x+7}{12x-11} = \dfrac{6x-39}{13x-21}$, then x is equal to

(a) $\dfrac{32}{25}, \dfrac{-18}{7}$ (b) $\dfrac{32}{15}, \dfrac{18}{7}$ (c) $\dfrac{32}{15}, \dfrac{8}{17}$ (d) None of these

Exercise 1

1. $4, \dfrac{1}{4}$ **2.** $\dfrac{1}{2}$ **3.** $\dfrac{63}{10}, \dfrac{-18}{35}$ **4.** $-\dfrac{5}{4}, -1$

5. $-\dfrac{5}{2}, 0$ **6.** $0, -2\dfrac{1}{2}$ **7.** $0, -\dfrac{61}{60}$ **8.** $0, \dfrac{-11}{2}$

9. $0, \dfrac{-31}{7}$ **10.** $0, -\dfrac{1392}{91}$

Exercise 2

1. (b) **2.** (b) **3.** (a) **4.** (c) **5.** (a)

13   Cubic Equations

To solve a cubic equation we can use vedic sutras "Lopanasthapanabhyam". "Paravartya Yojayet" and "Purna Apuranabhyam".

But "Purna Apuranabhyam" and "Paravartya Yojayet" are used to solve the cubic equations together.

To Solve Cubic Equation Using Purna and Paravartya

Vedic sutras "Purna Apuranabhyam" and "Paravartya Yojayet" are used simultaneously.

These vedic sutras are used to the cubic equation of the form $ax^3 + bx^2 + cx + d = 0$. First change the cubic equation in the form $t^3 + 3mt + n = 0$ and factorise n such that sum of its first factor and square of second factor is equal to $3m$ and solve this equation.

The procedure of this method is much clear in the following examples.

Example 1   *Solve* $x^3 + 6x^2 + 11x + 6 = 0$

Solution   We know that

$$(x + 2)^3 = x^3 + 6x^2 + 12x + 8$$

Now, $\qquad\qquad x^3 + 6x^2 + 11x + 6 = 0$

$\Rightarrow \qquad\qquad (x + 2)^3 - 12x - 8 + 11x + 6 = 0$

$\Rightarrow \qquad\qquad\qquad\qquad (x + 2)^3 = x + 2$

Let $\qquad\qquad\qquad\qquad t = (x + 2)$

$\therefore \qquad\qquad\qquad\qquad t^3 - t = 0$

$\Rightarrow \qquad\qquad\qquad t(t - 1)(t + 1) = 0$

$\Rightarrow \qquad\qquad\qquad t = 0,\ t = 1\ \ \text{or}\ \ t = -1$

$\Rightarrow \qquad\qquad\qquad x + 2 = 0,\ x + 2 = 1$

or $\qquad\qquad\qquad\qquad x + 2 = -1$

$\Rightarrow \qquad\qquad\qquad x = -2,\ x = -1,\ x = -3$

Example 2   *Factorise* $x^3 + 9x^2 + 24x + 16 = 0$

Solution   We know that $(x + 3)^3 = x^3 + 9x^2 + 27x + 27$

$\therefore \qquad\qquad\qquad x^3 + 9x^2 + 24x + 16 = 0$

$$\Rightarrow \quad (x+3)^3 - 27x - 27 + 24x + 16 = 0$$
$$\Rightarrow \quad (x+3)^3 - 3x - 11 = 0$$
$$\Rightarrow \quad (x+3)^3 - 3(x+3) - 2 = 0$$

Let
$$x + 3 = t$$
$$\therefore \quad t^3 - 3t - 2 = 0$$

Now, factorise 2 such that sum of one factor and square of another factor is equal to 3 ie, $3 = 1^2 + 2$

$$t^3 - (1^2 + 2)t - 2 = 0$$
$$\Rightarrow \quad t^3 - t - 2t - 2 = 0$$
$$\Rightarrow \quad t(t^2 - 1) - 2(t + 1) = 0$$
$$\Rightarrow \quad (t+1)\{t(t-1) - 2\} = 0$$
$$\Rightarrow \quad (t+1)(t^2 - t - 2) = 0$$
$$\Rightarrow \quad (t+1)(t+1)(t-2) = 0$$
$$\Rightarrow \quad (t+1)^2(t-2) = 0$$
$$\Rightarrow \quad t = -1 \quad \text{or} \quad t = 2$$
$$\Rightarrow \quad x + 3 = -1 \quad \text{or} \quad x + 3 = 2$$
$$\Rightarrow \quad x = -4 \quad \text{or} \quad x = -1$$

If the equation is of the form $x^3 + 3mx + n = 0$ and n cannot be divide into two factors such that sum of one factor and square of other factor is equal to 3m.

Then, let $x^3 = p^3 + q^3 + 3pqx$

On putting this value in given equation
$$(p^3 + q^3) + 3pqx + 3mx + n = 0$$
$$\Rightarrow \quad (3pq + 3m)x + (p^3 + q^3) + n = 0$$

Now, put
$$3pq + 3m = 0$$
then
$$x = p - \frac{m}{p}$$
$$\Rightarrow \quad p^6 + bp^3 - m^3 = 0$$
$$\Rightarrow \quad p^3 = \frac{-b \pm \sqrt{b^2 + 4m^3}}{2}$$
$$\Rightarrow \quad p = \left[\frac{-b \pm \sqrt{b^2 + 4m^3}}{2}\right]$$

Now, value of q can also be calculated.

Example 3 *Solve* $x^3 - 2x - 1 = 0$

Solution This equation of the form
$$x^3 + 3mx + n = 0$$

Here, 1 cannot be factorise in discussed procedure. So, let us assume that
$$x^3 = p^3 + q^3 + 3pqx$$

On putting this value in given equation, we get

$$p^3 + q^3 + 3pqx - 2x - 1 = 0$$

$$(3pq - 2)x + p^3 + q^3 - 1 = 0$$

$$3pq - 2 = 0$$

$$\Rightarrow \qquad q = \frac{2}{3p}$$

$$\therefore \qquad x = p + \frac{2}{3p}$$

$$\therefore \qquad p^3 + \left(\frac{2}{3p}\right)^3 - 1 = 0$$

$$\Rightarrow \qquad p^3 + \frac{8}{27p^3} - 1 = 0$$

$$\Rightarrow \qquad 27p^6 - 27p^3 + 8 = 0$$

$$\therefore \qquad p^3 = \frac{27 \pm \sqrt{(-27)^3 - 4 \times 27 \times 8}}{2 \times 27}$$

$$\Rightarrow \qquad p = \left(\frac{-9 \pm \sqrt{-15}}{18}\right)^{1/3}$$

and $$\qquad q = \frac{2}{3}\left(\frac{-9 \pm \sqrt{-15}}{18}\right)^{-1/3}$$

Special Types of Cubic Equations

We have classified some type of cubic equations which have discussed below.

Type I   Let the equation is

$$\frac{1}{ax + b} + \frac{1}{cx + d} = \frac{1}{ex + f} + \frac{1}{gx + h}$$

Here, $\qquad D_1 + D_2 = D_3 + D_4$

$\Rightarrow \qquad D_1 + D_2 = D_3 + D_4 = 0$

(using vedic sutra "Sunyam Samya Samuchchaya")

and $\qquad D_1 - D_2 = D_3 - D_4$

and $\qquad D_1 - D_2 = D_4 - D_3$

which give the another values of x.

Example 4   *Solve* $\dfrac{1}{2x - 5} + \dfrac{1}{8 - 3x} = \dfrac{1}{6x - 7} + \dfrac{1}{10 - 7x}$

Solution ∵ $D_1 = 2x - 5, D_2 = 8 - 3x, D_3 = 6x - 7$ and $D_4 = 10 - 7x$

Here, $\qquad D_1 + D_2 = 2x - 5 + 8 - 3x$

$$= 3 - x$$

and $\qquad D_3 + D_4 = 6x - 7 + 10 - 7x$

$$= 3 - x$$

$$\Rightarrow \qquad D_1 + D_2 = D_3 + D_4$$

$\therefore$ By "Sunyam Samya Samuchchaya."

$$3 - x = 0 \Rightarrow x = 3$$

Now, $\qquad D_1 - D_2 = D_3 - D_4$

$$(2x - 5) - (8 - 3x) = (6x - 7) - (10 - 7x)$$

$$\Rightarrow \qquad 2x - 5 - 8 + 3x = 6x - 7 - 10 + 7x$$

$$\Rightarrow \qquad 5x - 13 = 13x - 17$$

$$\Rightarrow \qquad 8x = 4 \Rightarrow x = \frac{1}{2}$$

Now, $\qquad D_1 - D_2 = D_4 - D_3$

$$\Rightarrow \qquad (2x - 5) - (8 - 3x) = (10 - 7x) - (6x - 7)$$

$$\Rightarrow \qquad 2x - 5 - 8 + 3x = 10 - 7x - 6x + 7$$

$$\Rightarrow \qquad 5x - 13 = 17 - 13x$$

$$\Rightarrow \qquad 18x = 30$$

$$\Rightarrow \qquad x = \frac{30}{18} = \frac{5}{3}$$

***Type* II** Let the equation is $\left\{ \dfrac{ax + b}{cx + d} \right\}^2 = \dfrac{eg + f}{gx + h}$

Here, $\qquad \{(ax + b) - (cx + d)\} = \{(ex + f) - (gx + h)\}$

So, solution is given by

$$(ax + b) - (cx + d) = 0$$

and other solution is given by the equation

$$(ax + b + cx + d)(gx + h) = (cx + d)^2$$

Example 5 *Solve* $\left(\dfrac{3x + 7}{x + 1} \right)^2 = \dfrac{5x + 8}{3x + 2}$

Solution Since, the given equation of the form

$$\left(\frac{ax + b}{cx + d} \right)^2 = \frac{ex + f}{gx + h}$$

$\therefore$ Here, $\qquad ax + b = 3x + 7$

$$cx + d = x + 1$$

$$ex + f = 5x + 8$$

and $\qquad gx + h = 3x + 2$

Now, one solution is given by

$$(3x + 7) - (x + 1) = 0$$

$$\Rightarrow \qquad 3x + 7 - x - 1 = 0$$

$$\Rightarrow \qquad 2x = -6$$

$$\Rightarrow \qquad x = -3$$

and other solution is given by

$$(3x + 7 + x + 1)(3x + 2) = (x + 1)^2$$

$$\Rightarrow \qquad (4x + 8)(3x + 2) = x^2 + 2x + 1$$

$$12x^2 + 32x + 16 = x^2 + 2x + 1$$

$$\Rightarrow \qquad 11x^2 + 30x + 15 = 0$$

$$\Rightarrow \qquad x = \frac{-30 \pm \sqrt{900 - 60 \times 11}}{22}$$

$$= \frac{-30 \pm 2\sqrt{60}}{22}$$

$$= \frac{-15 \pm \sqrt{60}}{11}$$

Type III Let the equation is

$$(x - m)^3 + (x - n)^3 = (x - m - p)^3 + (x - n + p)^3,$$

then,

$$x = -\frac{1}{2}(m + n)$$

(By using vedic sutra "Sunyam Samya Samuchchaya".)

Example 6 . *Solve* $(x - 59)^3 + (x - 21)^3 = (x - 34)^3 + (x - 46)^3$

Solution The given equation can be reduces as

$$(x - 59)^3 + (x - 21)^3 = (x - 59 + 25)^3 + (x - 21 - 25)^3$$

$$\therefore \qquad x = \frac{59 + 21}{2} = 40$$

Chapter Practice

Solve the following cubic equations.

1. $x^3 - 6x^2 + 11x - 6 = 0$

2. $x^3 + 6x^2 - 37x + 30 = 0$

3. $x^3 + 7x^2 + 14x + 8 = 0$

4. $x^3 + 8x^2 + 17x + 10 = 0$

5. $x^3 + 10x^2 + 27x + 18 = 0$

6. $x^3 + 9x^2 + 26x + 24 = 0$

7. $x^3 + 11x + 1 = 0$

8. $\dfrac{1}{x+3} + \dfrac{1}{4x+5} = \dfrac{1}{2x+7} + \dfrac{1}{3x+1}$

9. $\left(\dfrac{3x-5}{x-8}\right)^2 = \dfrac{3x+4}{x+1}$

10. $(x-7)^3 + (x-8)^3 = (x-9)^3 + (x-6)^2$

Answers

1. $x = 3, 1, 2$

2. $x = 1, 3, -10$

3. $x = -2, 4, 1$

4. $x = -2, -1, -5$

5. $x = -3, -6, -1$

6. $x = -3, -2, -4$

7. $x = p + q$, $p = \left(\dfrac{-9 \pm \sqrt{47997}}{18}\right)^{1/3}$, $q = \dfrac{-11}{\left(\dfrac{-9 \pm \sqrt{47997}}{18}\right)^{1/3}}$

8. $x = 1, -4, -8/5$

9. $x = -3/2, \dfrac{-7 \pm \sqrt{973}}{6}$

10. $x = \dfrac{15}{2}$

14 Biquadratic Equations

Biquadratic equations are those equations which are of degree 4. The vedic sutra "Purna" and "Paravartya Yojayet" are used to solve a biquadratic equations as a similar manner as for cubic equations.

We know that

$$(x + a)^4 = x^4 + 4x^3 a + 6x^2 a^2 + 4xa^3 + a^4$$

The proceduse is same as discussed in last chapter but may be much clear in the following example.

Example 1   *Solve* $x^4 + 8x^3 + 14x^2 - 8x - 15 = 0$

Solution   We know that,
$$(x + 2)^4 = x^4 + 8x^3 + 24x^2 + 32x + 16$$
$$\therefore \quad (x + 2)^4 - 24x^2 - 32x - 16 + 14x^2 - 8x - 15 = 0$$
$$\Rightarrow \qquad\qquad (x + 2)^4 - 10x^2 - 40x - 31 = 0$$
$$\Rightarrow \qquad\qquad (x + 2)^4 - 10(x + 2)^2 + 9 = 0$$
Let $\qquad\qquad\qquad x + 2 = t$
$$\therefore \qquad t^4 - 10t^2 + 9 \;\Rightarrow\; t = \pm 1 \text{ or } \pm 3$$
Hence, $\qquad\qquad x = -1, -3, +1 \text{ or } -3$

If the equation is of the form as
$$(x + m + n)^4 + (x + m - n)^4 = p$$
Let $\qquad\qquad x + m = y \text{ and solve it.}$

Example 2   *Solve the equation*
$$(x + 8)^4 + (x + 6)^4 = 82$$

Solution   The given equation can be reduces to
$$(x + 7 + 1)^4 + (x + 7 - 1)^4 = 82$$
Let $\qquad\qquad\qquad x + 2 = y$
$$\therefore \qquad\qquad (y + 1)^4 + (y - 1)^4 = 82$$
$$\Rightarrow \qquad\qquad y^4 + 6y^2 - 40 = 0$$
$$\Rightarrow \qquad\qquad (y^2 + 10)(y^2 - 4) = 0$$
$$\Rightarrow \qquad\qquad y = \pm 2, \pm\sqrt{-10}$$
$$\Rightarrow \qquad\qquad x = -5, -9, -7 \pm \sqrt{-10}$$

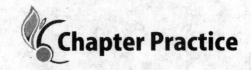

Chapter Practice

Solve the following Biquadratic equations.

1. $x^4 + 4x^3 - 25x^2 - 16x + 84 = 0$
2. $x^4 + 16x^3 + 86x^2 + 176x + 105 = 0$
3. $x^4 - 16x^3 + 91x^2 - 216x + 180 = 0$
4. $(x + 9)^4 + (x + 3)^3 = 882$
5. $(x + 7)^4 + (x + 5)^4 = 706$

Answers

1. $x = -2, 2, 3, -7$
2. $x = -3, -5, -1, -7$
3. $x = 3, 5, 6, 2$
4. $x = 6 \pm \sqrt{6}, 6 \pm \sqrt{-60}$
5. $x = 10, 2, -6 \pm \sqrt{-22}$

Simultaneous Equations

Simultaneous equations in two or more variables are solved by using Vedic sutra "Paravartya Yojayet" which means "Transpose and adjust". Also, by "Lopanasthapanabhyam".

But we have classified the types of simultaneous equations in following manner.

Type I Let the equations are

$$a_1 x + b_1 y = c_1$$

and

$$a_2 x + b_2 y = c_2$$

Then, by "Paravartya Yojayet"

$$x = \frac{b_1 c_2 - b_2 c_1}{a_2 b_1 - a_1 b_2}$$

and

$$y = \frac{a_2 c_1 - a_1 c_2}{a_2 b_1 - a_1 b_2}$$

Example 1 *Solve* $2x - 7y = 9$

$$4x - 3y = 5$$

Solution Here, $a_1 = 2, \ b_1 = -7, c_1 = 9$

$$a_2 = 4, b_2 = -3, c_2 = 5$$

Then, by vedic sutra "Paravartya Yojayet"

$$x = \frac{-7 \times 5 - (-3) \times 9}{4 \times (-7) - 2 \times (-3)}$$

$$= \frac{-35 + 27}{-28 + 6} = \frac{-8}{-22} = \frac{4}{11}$$

and

$$y = \frac{4 \times 9 - 2 \times 5}{4 \times (-7) - 2 \times (-3)}$$

$$= \frac{36 - 10}{-22}$$

$$= \frac{26}{-22} = \frac{-13}{11}$$

Hence,

$$x = \frac{4}{11}, y = \frac{-13}{11}$$

Type II Let the equations are

$$a_1 x + b_1 y = c_1$$

and $a_2 x + nb_1 y = nc_1$ such that $b_1 : nb_1 :: c_1 : nc_1$

Then, by vedic sutra "Anurupyena Sunyamanyat"

$$x = 0, y = \frac{c_1}{b_1}$$

Example 2 *Solve*

$$7x + 115y = 21$$
$$63x + 403y = 189$$

Solution ∵ $7 : 63 :: 21 : 189$

∴ $y = 0$

and $x = \dfrac{21}{7} = \dfrac{3}{1} = 3$

Type **III** Let the equations are

$$ax + by = c_1$$
$$bx + ay = c_2$$

first add these equations and one equation will be obtained which is named as (i), and now, subtract these equations and another equation will be obtained which is named as (ii). Now, solving Eqs (i) and (ii), we get the values of x and y.

Example 3 *Solve*

$$17x + 23y = 46 \qquad \qquad \text{...(i)}$$
$$23x + 17y = 34 \qquad \qquad \text{...(ii)}$$

Solution On adding Eqs. (i) and (ii), we get

$$40(x + y) = 80$$

⇒ $x + y = 2$ ...(iii)

Now, on subtracting Eq. (ii) from Eq. (i),

$$-6(x - y) = 12$$

⇒ $x - y = -2$ ...(iv)

On solving Eqs. (iii) and (iv), we get

$$x = 0 \quad \text{and} \quad y = 2$$

Type **IV** This type and solution can be clear in following example.

Example 4 *Solve* $x - y = 1$

and $xy = 110$

Solution By "Vilokanam"

$$x = 11 \text{ and } y = 10 \text{ or } x = -10 \text{ and } y = -11$$

These methods can be extended to three or more variables.

Chapter Practice

Exercise 1

Solve the following for x and y.

1. $2x + y = 5, 3x - 4y = 2$

2. $5x - 3y = 11, 6x - 5y = 9$

3. $12x + 8y = 7, 16x + 16y = 14$

4. $12x + 78y = 12, 16x + 16y = 16$

5. $517x + 91y = 455, 1023x + 13y = 65$

6. $45x - 23y = 113, 23x - 45y = 91$

7. $105x + 117y = 393, 117x + 105y = 273$

8. $3x + 4y = 30, xy = 12$

9. $x^3 - y^3 = 91, x - y = 1$

10. $2x + 3y - z = 1,$
    $x + 2y - 3z = 2,$
    $3x - y + 2z = 4$

Exercise 2

Solve the following for x and y.

1. $x - y = 3, 3x - 2y = 10$
   (a) $x = 4, y = 1$ (b) $x = 3, y = 2$
   (c) $x = 0, y = -3$ (d) None of these

2. $2x - 5y + 8 = 0, x - 4y + 7 = 0$
   (a) $x = 1, y = 1$ (b) $x = 1, y = 2$
   (c) $x = 4, y = 3$ (d) $x = 0, y = \dfrac{7}{4}$

3. $31x + 23y = 39,$
   $23x + 31y = 15$
   (a) $x = 2, y = -1$ (b) $x = 2, y = 1$
   (c) $x = 2, y = -2$ (d) $x = 2, y = -3$

4. $23x + 37y = 32,$
   $37x + 23y = 88$
   (a) $x = 2, y = 3$ (b) $x = 1\dfrac{1}{2}, y = \dfrac{1}{3}$
   (c) $x = 3, y = -1$ (d) None of these

5. $x + 3y = 17, 4x + 9y = 51$
   (a) $y = 0, x = 3$ (b) $x = 0, y = \dfrac{17}{3}$
   (c) $x = 0, y = 3$ (d) None of these

Answers

Exercise 1

1. $x = 2, y = 1$
2. $x = 4, y = 3$
3. $x = 0, y = 7/8$
4. $x = 1, y = 0$
5. $x = 0, y = 5$
6. $x = 2, y = -1$
7. $x = -7/2, y = 13/2$
8. $x = 8, y = 3/2$ or $x = 2, y = 6$
9. $x = 6, y = 5$ or $x = -5, y = -6$
10. $y = \dfrac{-23}{24}, x = \dfrac{37}{24}, z = \dfrac{-19}{24}$

Exercise 2

1. (a)   2. (b)   3. (a)   4. (c)   5. (b)

16 Factorization and Differential Calculus

"Gunita Samuchchaya" which means "The whole product is same" *ie*, if a quadratic expression is the product of two expressions $(a + b)$ and $(a + d)$, then its first differential is equal to the sum of these two expressions.

Example 1 Verify the Gunita Samuchchaya for the function
$$x^2 + 3x + 2$$

Solution ∵ $\qquad x^2 + 3x + 2 = (x + 1)(x + 2)$

Now, $\qquad \dfrac{d}{dx}(x^2 + 3x + 2) = 2x + 3$

Also, $\qquad x + 1 + x + 2 = 2x + 3$

∴ $\qquad \dfrac{d}{dx}(x^2 + 3x + 2) = (x + 1) + (x + 2)$

Thus, the sum of factors is equal to differential of product of factors.

Factorisation Using Differential Calculus

There is a closed relation between factorisation and differential calculus. We use this relation to identify the repeating factors by applying continuous differential which is discussed in the chapter 9.

17 Partial Fractions

To convert any rational fraction into different parts, we use vedic sutra "Paravartya Yojayet" which means "Transpose and Apply". The conventional method to find partial fractions is too long due to many number of steps and complicated calculations.

We divide the fractions in the following types
  (i) When denominator has no repeated terms.
  (ii) When order of numerator and denominator are same.
  (iii) When denominator has repeated terms.

When denominator has no repeated terms

We use the vedic sutra "Paravartya Yojayet" to find partial fraction. The procedure is explained in the following example.

Example 1 *Convert* $\dfrac{2x+3}{(x+1)(x+2)}$ *into partial fraction.*

Solution Let

$$\frac{2x+3}{(x+1)(x+2)} = \frac{A}{(x+1)} + \frac{B}{(x+2)}$$

Now, put $\qquad x+1=0$

$\Rightarrow \qquad\qquad\qquad x=-1$

$\therefore$ The value of $A = \dfrac{2\times(-1)+3}{(-1+2)} = \dfrac{-2+3}{1} = 1$

and now put $\qquad x+2=0$

$\Rightarrow \qquad\qquad x=-2$

$\therefore \quad$ The value of $B = \dfrac{2\times(-2)+3}{-2+1} = \dfrac{-4+3}{-1} = \dfrac{-1}{-1} = 1$

$\therefore \qquad \dfrac{2x+3}{(x+1)(x+2)} = \dfrac{1}{x+1} + \dfrac{1}{x+2}$

Example 2 *Convert* $\dfrac{2x+1}{x^3+6x^2+11x+6}$ *into partial fractions.*

Solution First in this question, factorise $x^3+6x^2+11x+6$ using vedic sutra "Purna"

$$x^3+6x^2+11x+6 = (x+1)(x+2)(x+3)$$

Let $\dfrac{2x+1}{(x+1)(x+2)(x+3)} = \dfrac{A}{x+1} + \dfrac{B}{x+2} + \dfrac{C}{x+3}$

Put $\qquad x+1=0$

$\Rightarrow \qquad x=-1$

∴ The value of $A = \dfrac{2\times(-1)+1}{(-1+2)(-1+3)} = \dfrac{-2+1}{1\times 2} = \dfrac{-1}{2}$

Now, put $x+2=0$

$\Rightarrow \qquad x=-2$

∴ The value of $B = \dfrac{2\times(-2)+1}{(-2+1)(-2+3)} = \dfrac{-4+1}{(-1)(1)} = 3$

and now, put $x+3=0$

$\Rightarrow \qquad x=-3$

∴ The value of $C = \dfrac{2\times(-3)+1}{(-3+1)(-3+2)} = \dfrac{-6+1}{(-2)(-1)} = \dfrac{-5}{2}$

Hence, $\dfrac{2x+1}{(x+1)(x+2)(x+3)} = \dfrac{-1}{2(x+1)} + \dfrac{3}{(x+2)} - \dfrac{5}{2(x+3)}$

The general formula is

For $\qquad \dfrac{lx^2+mx+n}{(x-a)(x-b)(x-c)} = \dfrac{A}{x-a} + \dfrac{B}{x-b} + \dfrac{C}{x-c}$

$$A = \dfrac{la^2+ma+n}{(a-b)(a-c)}, \; B = \dfrac{lb^2+mb+n}{(b-c)(b-a)} \; and$$

$$C = \dfrac{lc^2+mc+n}{(c-a)(c-b)}$$

When the order of numerator and denominator are same

When order of numerator and denominator are same, first we divide numerator by denominator to make improper fraction to proper fraction. But remaining process remains same.

Example 3 *Divide* $\dfrac{5x^2+9x-12}{x^2+x-42}$ *into partial fractions.*

Solution ∵ $\dfrac{5x^2+9x-12}{x^2+x-42} = 5 + \dfrac{4x+198}{x^2+x-42}$

Now, divide $\dfrac{4x+198}{x^2+x-42}$ into partial fractions.

$$\dfrac{4x+198}{(x+7)(x-6)} = \dfrac{A}{(x+7)} + \dfrac{B}{(x-6)}$$

Put $\qquad x+7=0$

$\Rightarrow \qquad x=-7$

$$\therefore \text{ The value of } A = \frac{4 \times (-7) + 198}{(-7 - 6)} = \frac{-28 + 198}{-13} = \frac{-170}{13}$$

Now,   put $x - 6 = 0 \;\; \Rightarrow \;\; x = 6$

$$\therefore \;\; \text{The value of } B = \frac{4 \times 6 + 198}{(6 + 7)} = \frac{222}{13}$$

Hence, $\dfrac{5x^2 + 9x - 217}{x^2 + x - 42} = 5 - \dfrac{170}{13\,(x + 7)} + \dfrac{222}{13\,(x - 6)}$

When denominator has repeated terms

When denominator has repeated terms, then the process of dividing into partial fractions is changed. The process is discussed in the following examples.

Example 4   *Divide $\dfrac{5x - 7}{(x - 3)^2}$ into partial fractions.*

Solution   Let $\dfrac{5x - 7}{(x - 3)^2} = \dfrac{A}{(x - 3)^2} + \dfrac{B}{(x - 3)}$

Put $x - 3 = 0$

$\Rightarrow$ $x = 3$

$\therefore$ $A = (5x - 7)_{\text{at } x = 3} = 5 \times 3 - 7 = 15 - 7 = 8$

Now, $B = \left[\dfrac{d}{dx}(5x - 7)\right]_{\text{at } x = 3} = 5$

Thus, $\dfrac{(5x - 7)}{(x - 3)^2} = \dfrac{8}{(x - 3)^2} + \dfrac{5}{x - 3}$

Example 5   *Divide $\dfrac{4x^2 + 6x - 9}{(x + 3)^3}$ into partial fractions.*

Solution $\dfrac{4x^2 + 6x - 9}{(x + 3)^3} = \dfrac{A}{(x + 3)^3} + \dfrac{B}{(x + 3)^2} + \dfrac{C}{(x + 3)}$

Put $x + 3 = 0 \;\; \Rightarrow \;\; x = -3$

$\therefore$ Value of $A = [4x^2 + 6x - 9]_{\text{at } x = -3}$

$$= 4 \times (-3)^2 + 6 \times (-3) - 9 = 36 - 18 - 9 = 9$$

$$\text{Value of } B = \frac{1}{1!}\left[\frac{d}{dx}(4x^2 + 6x - 9)\right]_{\text{at } x = -3}$$

$$= [8x + 6]_{\text{at } x = -3} = -24 + 6 = -18$$

and   Value of $C = \dfrac{1}{2!}\left[\dfrac{d^2}{dx^2}(4x^2 + 6x - 9)\right]_{\text{at } x = -3}$

$$= \frac{1}{2!}\left[\frac{d}{dx}(8x + 6)\right]_{\text{at } x = -3} = \frac{1}{2} \times 8 = 4$$

Hence, $\dfrac{4x^2 + 6x - 9}{(x + 3)^3} = \dfrac{9}{(x + 3)^3} - \dfrac{18}{(x + 3)^2} + \dfrac{4}{(x + 3)}$

Chapter Practice

Exercise 1

Divide the following into partial fractions.

1. $\dfrac{4x + 3}{(x - 1)(x + 2)}$

2. $\dfrac{x^3 + 9}{(x - 1)(x - 2)(x + 5)(x - 7)}$

3. $\dfrac{1}{(x + 1)(x + 3)(x + 5)}$

4. $\dfrac{x + 2}{x^2 - 4x + 3}$

5. $\dfrac{5x^2 + 9x - 217}{x^2 + x - 42}$

6. $\dfrac{2x^3 - 11x^2 + 12x + 1}{x^3 - 6x^2 + 11x - 6}$

7. $\dfrac{4x^2 + 6x - 9}{(x + 6)^3}$

8. $\dfrac{5 + 2x - 2x^2}{(x^2 - 1)(x + 1)}$

9. $\dfrac{5x^4 - 8x + 256}{x(x + 4)^4}$

10. $\dfrac{x^3 + 3x + 1}{(1 - x)^4}$

Exercise 2

Resolve the following into partial fraction.

1. $\dfrac{2x + 3}{x^2 - 2x - 3}$

(a) $\dfrac{9}{4(x + 3)} + \dfrac{1}{(x + 1)}$

(b) $\dfrac{9}{4(x - 3)} - \dfrac{1}{4(x + 1)}$

(c) $\dfrac{9}{4(x - 3)} - \dfrac{1}{(x + 1)}$

(d) None of these

2. $\dfrac{16}{(x - 2)(x + 2)^2}$

(a) $\dfrac{1}{x - 2} - \dfrac{1}{x + 2} - \dfrac{4}{(x + 2)^2}$

(b) $\dfrac{1}{x - 2} + \dfrac{1}{x + 2} - \dfrac{4}{(x + 2)^2}$

(c) $\dfrac{1}{x - 2} + \dfrac{1}{x + 2} - \dfrac{4}{(x + 2)^2}$

(d) None of these

3. $\dfrac{x^3 - 2x^2 - 13x - 12}{x^2 - 3x - 10}$

(a) $(x + 1) - \dfrac{2}{x - 5} + \dfrac{2}{7(x + 2)}$

(b) $(x + 1) - \dfrac{2}{7(x - 5)} + \dfrac{2}{7(x + 2)}$

(c) $\dfrac{2}{7(x - 5)} - \dfrac{2}{7(x + 2)}$

(d) None of these

4. $\dfrac{2x + 1}{(x - 1)(x^2 + 1)}$

(a) $\dfrac{3}{2(x - 1)} + \dfrac{1 + 3x}{2(x^2 + 1)}$

(b) $\dfrac{3}{2(x - 1)} + \dfrac{1 - 3x}{x^2 + 1}$

(c) $\dfrac{3}{2(x - 1)} - \dfrac{(1 - 3x)}{2(x^2 + 1)}$

(d) None of these

5. $\dfrac{x^2 + x + 1}{(x-1)^4}$

(a) $\dfrac{1}{(x-1)^2} + \dfrac{3}{(x-1)^3} + \dfrac{3}{(x-1)^4}$

(b) $\dfrac{1}{(x-1)^2} + \dfrac{3}{(x-1)^3} - \dfrac{3}{(x-1)^4}$

(c) $\dfrac{1}{(x-1)} + \dfrac{3}{(x-1)^2} - \dfrac{3}{(x-1)^3}$

(d) None of these

Answers

Exercise 1

1. $\dfrac{7}{3(x-1)} + \dfrac{5}{3(x+2)}$

2. $\dfrac{5}{18(x-1)} - \dfrac{17}{35(x-2)} + \dfrac{29}{126(x+5)} + \dfrac{44}{45(x-7)}$

3. $\dfrac{1}{8(x+1)} - \dfrac{1}{4(x+3)} + \dfrac{1}{8(x+5)}$

4. $-\dfrac{3}{2(x-1)} + \dfrac{5}{2(x-3)}$

5. $5 + \dfrac{35}{13(x+7)} + \dfrac{17}{13(x-6)}$

6. $2 + \dfrac{2}{x-1} + \dfrac{3}{x-2} - \dfrac{4}{x-3}$

7. $\dfrac{99}{(x+6)^3} - \dfrac{42}{(x+6)^2} + \dfrac{4}{(x+6)}$

8. $-\dfrac{1}{2(x+1)^2} - \dfrac{13}{4(x+1)} + \dfrac{5}{4(x-1)}$

9. $\dfrac{1}{x} - \dfrac{592}{(x+4)^4} + \dfrac{224}{(x+4)^3} - \dfrac{64}{(x+4)^2} + \dfrac{4}{x+4}$

10. $\dfrac{5}{(1-x)^4} - \dfrac{6}{(1-x)^3} + \dfrac{3}{(1-x)^2} - \dfrac{1}{(1-x)}$

Exercise 2

1. (b) 2. (a) 3. (b) 4. (d) 5. (a)

18 Integration by Partial Fractions

In order to find the integral of a power of x, we have to follow the following steps

Step I Add unity to the original index.

Divide the coefficient by the new index.

Add constant of integration to the resultant.

Example 1 *Integrate* $x^4 + 6x^3 + 3x^2 + 9x - 7$

Solution $\int (x^4 + 6x^3 + 3x^2 + 9x - 7)\,dx$

$$= \frac{x^{4+1}}{4+1} + \frac{6x^{3+1}}{3+1} + \frac{3x^{2+1}}{2+1} + \frac{9\,x^{1+1}}{1+1} - 7x + C$$

(where C is constant of integration)

$$= \frac{x^5}{5} + \frac{6}{4}x^4 + \frac{3}{3}x^3 + \frac{9}{2}x^2 - 7x + C = \frac{x^5}{5} + \frac{3}{2}x^4 + x^3 + \frac{9}{2}x^2 - 7x + C$$

This formula is in general form is given by $\int x^n dx = \frac{x^{n+1}}{n+1} + C$

and this formula is not applicable, if $n = -1$

$\because \qquad \int \frac{1}{x}\,dx = \log x + C$

Integration Using Partial Fraction

To integrate those functions which have numerator and denominator, we have to follow the following steps

Step I First find the factors of denominator even by using vedic sutra "Purna".

Step II Now, divide this function into partial fraction by using vedic sutra "Pravartya Yojayet."

Step III Integrate each partial fraction and add constant of integration. In integration we can use substitution.

Example 2 *Integrate* $\dfrac{7x - 1}{6x^2 - 5x + 1}$

Solution $\because \quad \dfrac{7x - 1}{6x^2 - 5x + 1} = \dfrac{5}{2x - 1} - \dfrac{4}{3x - 1}$

$\therefore \quad \int \dfrac{7x - 1}{6x^2 - 5x + 1}\,dx = \int \left\{ \dfrac{5}{2x - 1} - \dfrac{4}{3x - 1} \right\} dx$

$$= \frac{5}{2} \log(2x - 1) - \frac{4}{3} \log(3x - 1) + C = \log \frac{(2x - 1)^{5/2}}{(3x - 1)^{4/3}} + C$$

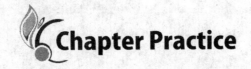

Chapter Practice

Integrate the following functions.

1. $(2x + 1)^3$

2. $(x^6 + 1)$

3. $x^2 + 5x + 6$

4. $ax^{-2} + bx^{-1} + C$

5. $x^2 + x - 6$

6. $3x^2 + 2x$

7. $\dfrac{1}{(x - x^2)}$

8. $\dfrac{1}{(x + 1)(x + 2)}$

9. $\dfrac{1}{(x - 1)(x^2 + 1)}$

10. $\dfrac{x^2 + x - 1}{x^2 + x - 6}$

11. $\dfrac{x}{x^4 - 1}$

12. $\dfrac{1}{x(x^7 + 1)}$

Answers

1. $\dfrac{(2x + 1)^4}{8} + C$

2. $\dfrac{x^7}{7} + x + C$

3. $\dfrac{x^3}{3} + \dfrac{5x}{2} + 6x + C$

4. $-ax^{-1} + b \log x + cx + d$

5. $\dfrac{x^3}{3} + \dfrac{x^2}{2} - 6x + C$

6. $x^3 + x^2 + C$

7. $\log x - \log(1 - x) + C$

8. $\log \dfrac{x + 1}{x + 2} + C$

9. $\dfrac{1}{2} \log(x - 1) - \dfrac{1}{4} \log(x^2 + 1) - \dfrac{1}{2} \tan^{-1} x + C$

10. $x - \log(x + 3) + \log(x - 2) + C$

11. $\dfrac{1}{4} \log\left(\dfrac{x^2 - 1}{x^2 + 1}\right) + C$

12. $\dfrac{1}{7} \log\left(\dfrac{x^7}{x^7 + 1}\right) + C$

19 Pythagoras Theorem

We are here to describe this topic, not to use this topic but to show you that this theorem is well known to Indians before Pythagoras.

This theorem has an important use in trigonometry, analytical geometry differential calculus etc.

The following two descriptions shows that Pythagoras Theorem is well known to us.

Ist Proof

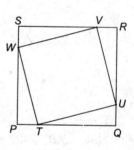

Let
$$PT = UQ = RV = SW$$
and
$$TQ = UR = SV = WP$$
$$SQ^2 = UW^2$$
$$+ \text{ 4 congruent right angled triangles}$$

$$\therefore \quad WT^2 + 4\left(\frac{1}{2} \times WP \times PT\right) = (WP + PT)^2$$

$$\Rightarrow \quad WT^2 + 2 \times WP \times PT = WP^2 + PT^2 + 2\,WP \times PT$$

$$\Rightarrow \quad WT^2 = WP^2 + PT^2$$

IInd Proof

We know that if $\triangle ABC$, ABD and BCA are similar

$$\therefore \quad \frac{AB^2}{AC^2} = \frac{\text{area}\,(\triangle ABD)}{\text{area}(\triangle ABC)} \qquad \text{...(i)}$$

and
$$\frac{BC^2}{AC^2} = \frac{\text{area}\,(\triangle BCD)}{\text{area}\,(\triangle ABC)} \qquad \text{...(ii)}$$

On adding Eqs. (i) and (ii), we get

$$\frac{AB^2}{AC^2} + \frac{BC^2}{AC^2} = \frac{\text{area}\,(\triangle ABD)}{\text{area}\,(\triangle ABC)} + \frac{\text{area}\,(\triangle BCD)}{\text{area}\,(\triangle ABC)}$$

$$\Rightarrow \quad \frac{AB^2 + BC^2}{AC^2} = \frac{\text{area}\,(\triangle ABD) + \text{area}\,(\triangle BCD)}{\text{area}\,(\triangle ABC)}$$

$$= \frac{\text{area}\,(\triangle ABC)}{\text{area}\,(\triangle ABC)} = 1$$

$$\Rightarrow \quad AB^2 + BC^2 = AC^2$$

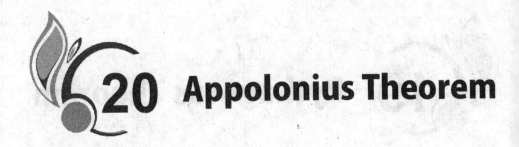

20 Appolonius Theorem

Appolonius theorem is elementary corollary of Pythagoras theorem. We are here with its proof with help of Vedic Mathematics.

To Prove

In $\triangle ABC$, if D is mid point of BC, then,

$$AB^2 + AC^2 = 2(AD^2 + BD^2)$$

Proof Let AE is perpendicular to BC.

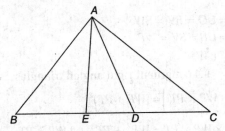

Now, $\begin{aligned}[t] AB^2 + AC^2 &= AE^2 + BE^2 + AE^2 + EC^2 \qquad \text{(In } \triangle^s \ ABE \text{ and } AEC) \\ &= 2AE^2 + (BD - ED)^2 + (CD + ED)^2 \\ &= 2AE^2 + BD^2 + ED^2 - 2BD \cdot ED + CD^2 + ED^2 + 2CD \cdot ED \\ &= 2AE^2 + 2ED^2 + 2BD^2 - 2BD \cdot ED + 2BD \cdot ED \qquad (\because CD = BD) \\ &= 2(AE^2 + ED^2) + 2BD^2 \\ &= 2AD^2 + 2BD^2 \qquad (\because \text{In } \triangle AED, AD^2 = AE^2 + ED^2) \end{aligned}$

Hence, $AB^2 + AC^2 = 2(AD^2 + BD^2)$

21 Analytical Geometry

This is a branch of Mathematics which is related to othere branches.
Some important uses of Vedic Maths are as follows.

Equation of Straight Line

The equation of straight line passing through (x_1, y_1) and (x_2, y_2) by using "Paravartya Yojayet" can be found by follow the following steps.

Step 1 Find $y_2 - y_1$ which is coefficient of x.

Step 2 Find $x_2 - x_1$ which is coefficient of y. Now, left side of equation is

$$(y_2 - y_1)x - (x_2 - x_1)y$$

Step 3 Substitute x and y by x_1 and y_1 or by x_2 and y_2 respectively which gives the right side of equation.

Thus, equation of straight line is

$$(y_2 - y_1)x - (x_2 - x_1)y$$
$$= (y_2 - y_1)x_1 - (x_2 - x_1)y_1$$

Example 1 *Find the equation of straight line passing through* $(10, 5)$ *and* $(18, 9)$.

Solution Here, $x_1 = 10$, $y_1 = 5$ and $x_2 = 18$, $y_2 = 9$

$\therefore$ Coefficient of $x = y_2 - y_1 = 9 - 5 = 4$

and coefficient of $y = x_2 - x_1 = 18 - 10 = 8$

$\therefore$ Left side of equation is

$$(y_2 - y_1)x - (x_2 - x_1)y = 4x - 8y$$

and right side $= 4 \times x_1 - 8 \times y_1$

$= 4 \times 10 - 8 \times 5 = 0$

Hence, equation of straight line is

$$4x - 8y = 0$$

or $$x - 2y = 0$$

Pair of Straight Lines

To find that the given equation $ax^2 + 2hxy + by^2 + 2gx + 2fy + c = 0$ represents a pair of straight line, we use vedic sutras "Urdhava Triyagbhyam" and "Lopanasthapanabhyam". whose meaning are "transpose and apply" and "by alternate elimination and retention" respectively.

The process is described in following example.

Example 2 *Show that the equation*
$$12x^2 + 7xy - 10y^2 + 13x + 45y - 35 = 0$$
represents a pair of straight line.

Solution By using "Urdhava Triyak Method, "Lopanasthapanabhyam" we can say that
$$12x^2 + 7xy - 10y^2 = (3x - 2y)(4x + 5y)$$

and 7 and −5 are two absolute values.

Thus, equation of lines are
$$3x - 2y + 7 = 0 \quad \text{and} \quad 4x + 5y - 5 = 0$$

Equation of Asymptotes of a Hyperbola

The equation of asymptotes and conjugate hyperbola we use vedic sutra "Paravartya Yojayet", "Lopanasthapanabhyam", and "Aadhyamadhya Nantanyamntyen".

The procedure of explanation is as follows which is decribed in following example.

Example 3 *Find the equation of asymptote and conjugate of hyperbola*
$$8x^2 + 10xy - 3y^2 - 2x + 4y - 2 = 0.$$

Solution The given equation can be rewritten using vedic sutras as
$$(2x + 3y)(4x - y) - 2x + 4y - 2 = 0$$
$$\therefore \quad (4x - y + 1)(2x + 3y - 1)$$
$$= 8x^2 + 10xy - 3y^2 - 2x + 4y - 1$$

An equation of asymptotes is
$$8x^2 + 10xy - 3y^2 - 2x + 4y - 1 = 0$$

and equation of conjugate hyperbola is
$$8x^2 + 10xy - 3y^2 - 2x + 4y = 0$$

Chapter Practice

1. Find the equation of straight line passing through
   (i) $(4, 7)$ and $(3, 5)$ (ii) $(17, 9)$ and $(13, -8)$

2. Show that the following equation represents a pair of straight line.
   (i) $2x^2 + 7xy + 3y^2 + 8x + y + 8 = 0$
   (ii) $3x^2 + 10xy + 3y^2 - 15x - 21y + 18 = 0$

3. Find the equation of asymptotes and conjugate hyperbola of hyperbola.
   (i) $y^2 - xy - 2x^2 - 5y + x - 6 = 0$
   (ii) $55x^2 - 120xy + 20y^2 + 64x - 48y = 0$

Answers

1. (i) $2x - y = 1$ (ii) $17x - 4y = 253$
3. (i) $y^2 - xy - 2x^2 + x - 5y + 6 = 0$ and $y^2 - xy - 2x^2 + x - 5y + 18 = 0$
   (ii) $55x^2 - 120xy + 20y^2 + 64x - 48y + 16 = 0$
   and $55x^2 - 120xy + 20y^2 + 64x - 48y + 32 = 0$

Hints & Solutions

Hints & Solutions

1 : Addition

Exercise 2

1.
```
  3 5 9 6
  2 1 2 3
+ 5 4 7 2
---------
1 1 1 9 1
```

2.
```
  5 8 3 2 1
+ 6 9 3 8 6
-----------
1 2 7 7 0 7
```

```
1 2 7 7 0 7
- 0 3 7 0 9 8
-----------
  9 0 7 0 9
```

3.
```
  1 8 3 4
+ 2 4 5 8
---------
  4 2 9 2
```

4.
```
  1 5 3 6 8
+   8 1 5 3
-----------
  2 3 5 2 1
```

5.
```
  3 4 1 2
  4 3 6 7
+ 5 5 9 0
---------
1 3 3 6 9
```

6.
```
  5 5 5 5
    5 5 5
      5 5
---------
  6 1 6 5
```

7.
```
  7 4 1 4
  3 6 9 8
  1 2 5 7
+ 1 8 6 9
---------
1 4 2 3 8
```

8.
```
  8 4 8 4
  4 2 4 8
  2 1 1 2
  1 0 7 4
+ 5 1 3
---------
1 6 4 3 1
```

9. Polynomials   Coefficients of variable

   $x^3 + x + 1$ 1 0 1 1

   $6x^2 + 5$ 0 6 0 5
                               ----
                                   1 6 1 6

   ∴ Resultant polynomial is $x^3 + 6x^2 + x + 6$.

10. Polynomials   Coefficients of variable

    $x + 3$ 0 0 1   3

    $x^3 + 9x^2 + 11x + 7$ 1 9 11   7
                              ----
                               1 9 (12) (10)

    ∴ Resultant polynomial is $x^3 + 9x^2 + 12x + 10$.

2 : Subtraction

Exercise 2

1.
```
  5 4 3
+ 1 1 1
-------
  6 5 4
```

```
  6 1 5 8
- 0 6 5 4
---------
  5 5 0 4
```

2.
```
  9 9 5
+   8 4
-------
1 0 7 9
```

```
  1 0 7 9
- 0 6 1 8
---------
  0 4 6 1
```

3. 8 1 5 3
    1 4 9 2
   + 6 1 7 5
   ———————
    1 5 8 2 0

∴ $8153 + 1492 = x - 6175 \Rightarrow x = 8153 + 1492 + 6175 = 15820$

4. 4 5 0 9 9   9 8 6 7 8
   + 1 0 0 3 6   − 5 5 1 3 5
   ———————   ———————
    5 5 1 3 5   4 3 5 4 3

5. 6 8 1 5   1 0 3 5 4
   + 1 3 5 9   − 0 8 1 7 4
   ———————   ———————
    8 1 7 4   0 2 1 8 0

6. 5 8 3 2 1   1 2 7 7 0 7
   + 6 9 3 8 6   − 0 3 7 0 9 8
   ———————   ———————
    1 2 7 7 0 7   9 0 6 0 9

         $58321 + 69386 = x + 37098 \Rightarrow 127707 = x + 37098$

$\Rightarrow$ $x = 127707 - 37098 = 90609$

7. 9 8 7 9
   − 1 3 5 8
   ———————
    8 5 2 1

        $9879 - x = 1358 \Rightarrow x = 9879 - 1358 = 8521$

8. $-31 - 35 - 37 + 18 + 17 = -31 - 35 - 37 + 35 = -31 - 37 = -68$

9. 5 9 8 2   4 5 8 8   8 0 6 3
    1 3 4 5   + 9 9 2   − 5 5 8 0
   + 7 3 6   ———————   ———————
   ———————   5 5 8 0   2 6 8 3
    8 0 6 3

$5982 + 1345 + 736 - x = 4588 + 992 \Rightarrow 8063 - x = 5580 \Rightarrow x = 8063 - 5580 = 2683$

10. 8 8 8 8   7 3 3 7   9 8 2 4
     8 4 8   + 7 3 7   − 8 0 7 4
    + 8 8   ———————   ———————
   ———————   8 0 7 4   1 7 5 0
    9 8 2 4

$8888 + 848 + 88 - x = 7337 + 737 \Rightarrow 9824 - x = 8074 \Rightarrow x = 9824 - 8074 = 1750$

3 : Multiplication

Exercise 2

1. We Know that,

$$abc$$
$$\times def$$
—————————————————————————————————————
$$(a \times d) / (a \times e + b \times d) / (a \times f + b \times e + c \times d) / (b \times f + c \times e) / (c \times f)$$

∴ 495×038

           $abc \quad def$

           $= 0 / 4 \times 3 / (4 \times 8 + 9 \times 3 + 5 \times 0) / (9 \times 8 + 5 \times 3) / (5 \times 8)$

$$= 12/59/87/40$$
$$= 12/59/91/0$$
$$= 12/68/10 = 18810$$

$\therefore \quad 495 \times 038 - 1885 = 18810 - 1885 = 16925$

```
  1 8 8 1 0
  • • •
-   1 8 8 5
  1 6 9 2 5
```

2. $180 \times 18 \times 8 = 180 \times 144$

$\qquad abc \quad def$

$= (1 \times 1)/(1 \times 4 + 8 \times 1)/(1 \times 4 + 8 \times 4 + 0)/(8 \times 4 + 0)/0$

$= 1/12/36/32/0 = 1/12/39/20 = 1/15/920 = 25920$

Now, $\quad 180 \times 18 \times 8 - 8888 = 25920 - 8888 = 17032$

```
  2 5 9 2 0
  • • •
- 0 8 8 8 8
  1 7 0 3 2
```

3. 555×061

$abc \quad def$

$= 0/(5 \times 6 + 0)/(5 \times 1 + 5 \times 6 + 0)/(5 \times 1 + 5 \times 6)/(5 \times 1)$

$= 30/35/35/5 = 30/38/55 = 33855$

$\therefore \qquad 555 \times 61 = 33855 - 25000 = 8855$

4. $338 \times 097 = 0/27/48/93/56$

$abc \quad def$

$= 27/48/98/6 = 27/57/86 = 32786$

$\therefore 338 \times 97 - 1835 = 32786 - 1835 = 30951$

```
  3 3 8 5 5
  •
- 2 5 0 0 0
  0 8 8 5 5
```

5. $150 \times 012 = 0/1/7/10/0$

$abc \quad def$

$\qquad = 1800$

$\therefore \qquad 15 + 150 \times 12 = 15 + 1800 = 1815$

```
  3 2 7 8 6
  •
-   1 8 3 5
  3 0 9 5 1
```

6. $120 \times (2 + 12) = 120 \times 14$

$\qquad = 120 \times 014$

$\qquad abc \quad def$

$\qquad = 0/1/6/8/0 = 1680$

7. $(15 + 15) \times 20 = 30 \times 20 = 600$

8.
```
  995   005
  997   003
  992   015
```

$\therefore \quad 995 \times 997 = 992015$

6 : Square and Square Root

Exercise 2

1. Nearest base is 70, which is 7 times of 10.

   Surplus of a number $= 71 - 70 = 1$

   Left block of resultant $= 7 \times (71 + 1) = 7 \times 72 = 504$

   and right block of resultant $= 1^2 = 1$

   Thus, $\qquad (71)^2 = 5041$

2. $(2.5)^2 = \left(\dfrac{25}{10}\right)^2 = \dfrac{2 \times (2 + 1)/25}{100} = \dfrac{625}{100} = 6.25$

3. $(16)^2 + (16)^2 = 2 \times (16)^2$

$$= 2 \times \{(16 + 6)/36\} = 2 \times (22/36)$$
$$= 2 \times 256 = 512$$

4. $9408 \div \sqrt{x} = 336$

$$\Rightarrow \qquad \sqrt{x} = \frac{9408}{336} \quad \Rightarrow \quad x = \left(\frac{9408}{336}\right)^2$$
$$= (28)^2 = 3(28 - 2)/(02)^2 = 3 \times 26/04 = 784$$

5. $\qquad\qquad 1254 + 1147 = x^2$

$$\Rightarrow \qquad\qquad x^2 = 2401$$
$$\Rightarrow \qquad\qquad x = \sqrt{2401} = \sqrt{7 \times 7 \times 7 \times 7} = 7 \times 7 = 49$$

6. $\qquad\qquad \sqrt{x} + 25 = \sqrt{5329}$

$$\Rightarrow \qquad\qquad \sqrt{x} + 25 = 73$$
$$\Rightarrow \qquad\qquad \sqrt{x} = 73 - 25 = 48$$
$$\Rightarrow \qquad\qquad x = (48)^2 = 5(48 - 2)/(2)^2 = 5 \times 46/4 = 2304$$

7. Since, nearest perfect square number to 3333 is 3364.

∴ Required number = 3364 − 3333 = 31

8. $\qquad\qquad \sqrt{x} - 18 = \sqrt{1444}$

$$\Rightarrow \qquad\qquad \sqrt{x} = 38 + 18 = 56$$
$$\Rightarrow \qquad\qquad x = (56)^2 = 6(56 - 4)/16 = 312/16 = 3136$$

9. $\qquad\qquad 79296 \div \sqrt{x} = 112 \times 12$

$$\Rightarrow \qquad\qquad \sqrt{x} = \frac{79296}{112 \times 12}$$
$$\Rightarrow \qquad\qquad x = (59)^2 = 6(59 - 1)/01 = 348/1 = 3481$$

10. Let the number be x, then

$$(51)^2 + x^2 = 15826$$
$$\Rightarrow \qquad\qquad x^2 = 15826 - (51)^2 = 15826 - 5(51 + 1)/1$$
$$= 15826 - 2601 = 13225$$
$$\Rightarrow \qquad\qquad x = \sqrt{13225} = 115$$

11. $\qquad\qquad 48096 \div \sqrt{x} = 167 \times 9$

$$\Rightarrow \qquad\qquad \sqrt{x} = \frac{48096}{167 \times 9} = 32$$
$$\Rightarrow \qquad\qquad x = (32)^2 = 3(32 + 2)/4 = 1024$$

12. $\qquad\qquad \sqrt{x} + 28 = \sqrt{1681}$

$$\Rightarrow \qquad\qquad \sqrt{x} + 28 = 41$$
$$\Rightarrow \qquad\qquad \sqrt{x} = 41 - 28 = 13$$
$$\Rightarrow \qquad\qquad x = (13)^2 = 169$$

13. Since, nearest perfect square number to 8200 is 8281.

∴ Required number = 8281 − 8200 = 81

14. Let the number be x.

$$\therefore \qquad (49)^2 + x^2 = 9125$$
$$\Rightarrow \qquad x^2 = 9125 - (49)^2$$
$$= 9125 - 5(49-1)/1$$
$$= 9125 - 2401 = 6724$$
$$\Rightarrow \qquad x = \sqrt{6724} = 82$$

15. $(64)^2 \div 8^2 = x^2$

$$\Rightarrow \qquad x^2 = \frac{64 \times 64}{8 \times 8} = 64 \qquad \Rightarrow \qquad x = \sqrt{64} = 8$$

16. $((13)^4)^{1/2} = (13)^2 = 169$

17. $\sqrt{2704} = \sqrt{13 \times 13 \times 2 \times 2 \times 2 \times 2} = 13 \times 4 = 52$

18. $\dfrac{\sqrt{4096} \times 56}{764 - 652} = \dfrac{64 \times 56}{112} = \dfrac{3584}{112} = 32$

19. $(94)^2 = (94-6)/36 = 88/36 = 8836$

$$(145)^2 = 14 \times 15/25 = 21025$$

and $$(56)^2 = 5(56+6)/36$$

$$= 310/36 = 3136$$

$$\therefore \qquad (94)^2 + x^2 = (145)^2 - (56)^2 - 3869$$
$$\Rightarrow \qquad x^2 = 21025 - 3136 - 3869 - 8836$$
$$= 21025 - 15841 = 5184$$
$$\Rightarrow \qquad x = \sqrt{5184} = 72$$

$$\begin{array}{r} 3\ 1\ 3\ 6 \\ 3\ 8\ 6\ 9 \\ +\ 8\ 8\ 3\ 6 \\ \hline 1\ 5\ 8\ 4\ 1 \end{array}$$

20. $\because \dfrac{2432}{x} = \sqrt{23104}$

$$\Rightarrow \qquad x = \frac{2432}{152} = 16$$

21. $\because$

$$(123)^2 = (123+23)/529$$
$$= 146/529 = 15129$$
$$(246)^2 = 4(123)^2 = 4 \times 15129 = 60516$$

and $$(99)^2 = (99-1)/01 = 9801$$

$$\therefore \qquad x^2 + (123)^2 = (246)^2 - (99)^2 - 2462$$
$$\Rightarrow \qquad x^2 = 60516 - 9801 - 15129 - 2462$$
$$= 33124$$
$$\Rightarrow \qquad x = \sqrt{33124} = 182$$

22. $[(84)^2 \div 28 \times 12] \div 24 = 7 \times x$

$$\Rightarrow \qquad x = \frac{84 \times 84 \times 12}{7 \times 28 \times 24} = 18$$

23. $\sqrt{x} = (88 \times 42) \div 16 = \dfrac{88 \times 42}{16} = 231$

$$\Rightarrow \qquad x = (231)^2 = 53361$$

24. $\sqrt{\sqrt{2500} + \sqrt{961}} = x^2$

$\Rightarrow \qquad\qquad\qquad\qquad \sqrt{50 + 31} = x^2$

$\Rightarrow \qquad\qquad\qquad\qquad 9 = x^2 \quad \Rightarrow \quad x = 3$

25. $\sqrt{915849} + \sqrt{795664} = x^2$

$\Rightarrow \qquad\qquad\qquad 957 + 892 = x^2$

$\Rightarrow \qquad\qquad 1849 = x^2 \quad \Rightarrow \quad x = \sqrt{1849} = 43$

26. $\sqrt{117649} = 343$

27. $\sqrt{248 + \sqrt{52 + \sqrt{144}}} = \sqrt{248 + \sqrt{52 + 12}} = \sqrt{248 + 8}$

$\qquad\qquad = \sqrt{256} = 16$

28. $\qquad (?)^2 = 28 \times 112$

$\qquad\qquad = 7 \times 2 \times 2 \times 2 \times 2 \times 7 \times 2 \times 2$

$\Rightarrow \qquad ? = 7 \times 2 \times 2 \times 2 = 56$

29. $\because \quad x = 15$ and $y = 20$

$\therefore \qquad\qquad\qquad\qquad \sqrt{x^2 + y^2} = \sqrt{15^2 + 20^2}$

$\qquad\qquad\qquad\qquad\qquad = \sqrt{225 + 400}$

$\qquad\qquad\qquad\qquad\qquad = \sqrt{625} = 25$

30. Let the number of students in the class be x.

$\therefore \qquad\qquad\qquad\qquad x^2 = 576$

$\Rightarrow \qquad\qquad\qquad\qquad x = \sqrt{576} = 24$

7 : Cube and Cube Root

Exercise 2

1. $\because \qquad\qquad (13)^3 = 3 \times 2 + 13 / 9 \times 3 / 3^3$

$\qquad\qquad\qquad = 19 / 27 / 27 = 19 / 29 / 7 = 2197$

and $\qquad\qquad (13)^2 = (13 + 3)/9 = 169$

$\therefore \qquad\qquad (13)^3 - (13)^2 = 2197 - 169 = 2028$

2. $\because \qquad\qquad\qquad 9^3 = -1 \times 2 + 9 / (-3) \times (-1) / (-1)^3 = 7 / 3 / -1$

$\qquad\qquad\qquad = 7 / 2 / (10 - 1) = 729$

$\therefore \qquad 1152 \div 36 + 9^3 = \dfrac{1152}{36} + 729$

$\qquad\qquad\qquad = 32 + 729$

$\qquad\qquad\qquad = 761$

3. Let the number be x.

$\therefore \qquad\qquad (14)^3 + x^2 = 4425$

But $\qquad\qquad (14)^3 = 4 \times 2 + 14 / (-2) \times 4 / 64 = 22 / (-8) / 64 = 2744$

$\Rightarrow \qquad\qquad x^2 = 4425 - 2744 = 1681$

$\Rightarrow \qquad\qquad x = \sqrt{1681} = 41$

4. $\because$
$$(45)^3 = 4^3 / 3 \times 4^2 \times 5 / 3 \times 4 \times 5^2 / 5^3$$
$$= 64 / 240 / 300 / 125$$
$$= 64 / 240 / 312 / 5$$
$$= 64 / 271 / 25$$
$$= 91125$$
$$(3320)^2 = 11022400$$

$\therefore$ $(45)^3 \times (11)^2 - (3320)^2 = 91125 \times 121 - 11022400$
$$= 11026125 - 11022400$$
$$= 3725$$

5. Let the number be x.

$\therefore$ $\qquad x^2 - (20)^3 = 4321$

$\Rightarrow$ $\qquad x^2 = 4321 + 8000 = 12321$

$\Rightarrow$ $\qquad x = \sqrt{12321} = 111$

6. $\qquad (36)^3 = 3^3 / 3 \times 3^2 \times 6 / 3 \times 3 \times 6^2 / 6^3$
$$= 27 / 162 / 324 / 216$$
$$= 27 / 162 / 345 / 6 = 27 / 196 / 56 = 46656$$
$$5^3 = 125$$

and $\qquad (2400)^2 = (24)^2 \times 10000$
$$= 5760000$$

$\therefore$ $\qquad (36)^3 \times 5^3 - (2400)^2 = 46656 \times 125 - (2400)^2$
$$= 5832000 - 5760000 = 72000$$

7. $\sqrt[3]{13824} \times \sqrt{x} = 864$

$\Rightarrow$ $\qquad \sqrt{x} = \dfrac{864}{24} \quad \Rightarrow \quad x = (36)^2$
$$= 1296$$

8. $\qquad \sqrt[3]{x} = \dfrac{756 \times 67}{804} = 63$

$\Rightarrow$ $\qquad x = (63)^3 = 6^3 / 3 \times 6^2 \times 3 / 3 \times 6 \times 3^2 / 3^3$
$$= 216 / 324 / 162 / 27$$
$$= 250047$$

9. $\sqrt[3]{4096} = \sqrt[3]{16 \times 16 \times 16} = 16$

10. $\sqrt[3]{1092727} = \sqrt[3]{103 \times 103 \times 103} = 103$

By inspection units place digit 7 can be possible only if unit's place digit in square root is 3. Which is only in option (b).

11. $\sqrt[3]{658503} = \sqrt[3]{87 \times 87 \times 87} = 87$

12. In given options only for option (b) 300, the resultant will be 27000 which is a perfect cube.

Thus, $\qquad A = 300$

13. $\because 1497375 = 11 \times 3 \times 5 \times 11 \times 11 \times 5 \times 5 \times 3$

Thus, on multiplying the given number by 3, then resultant will be a perfect cube.

14. $\because$ $1440 = 4 \times 4 \times 3 \times 3 \times 2 \times 5$

Thus, this number should be multiplied by $2 \times 3 \times 25$ ie, 150, the resultant will be a perfect cube. Hence, required sum $= 1 + 5 + 0 = 6$.

15. $\dfrac{\sqrt[3]{8}}{\sqrt{16}} \div \sqrt{\dfrac{100}{49}} \times \sqrt[3]{125} = \dfrac{2}{4} \times \dfrac{7}{10} \times 5 = \dfrac{7}{4} = 1\dfrac{3}{4}$

8 : Decimals

Exercise 2

1. $16 \times 36 \div 15 + 11 = \{1 \times 3 / (1 \times 6 + 6 \times 3) / 6 \times 6\} \div 15 + 11$

$= \{3 / 24 / 36\} \div 15 + 11$

$= 576 \div 15 + 11 = 38.4 + 11$

$= 49.4$

2. $38.7 \times 14.5 \times 6.4 = 38.7 \times 92.8$

$= 3591.36$ $(\because 145 \times 064 = 9280)$

3. $6.8 \times 8.8 \times 11.9 - 202.596 = 59.84 \times 11.9 - 202.596$

$= 712.096 - 202.596 = 509.5$

4.
$$
\begin{array}{r}
5\overset{\bullet}{5}6.\overset{\bullet}{6}\overset{\bullet}{5} \\
6\,5.6\,5 \\
5\,6.6\,5 \\
\hline
678.95
\end{array}
$$

Thus, $556.65 + 65.65 + 56.65 = 678.95$

5. $16.4 \times x = 590.4$

$\Rightarrow$ $x = \dfrac{5904}{164} = 36$

6. $\because$
$$
\begin{array}{r}
12\overset{\bullet}{7}\overset{\bullet}{6}.34 \\
+\,217.84 \\
\hline
1494.18
\end{array}
$$
$$
\begin{array}{r}
\overset{\bullet}{} \\
-\,0\,783.11 \\
\hline
0711.07
\end{array}
$$

$\therefore$ $1276.34 - 783.11 + 217.84 = 711.07$

7. $\because$ $9.3 \times x = 523.59$

$\Rightarrow$ $x = \dfrac{523.59}{9.3} = 56.3$

8.
$$
\begin{array}{r}
4\overset{\bullet}{3}.3\overset{\bullet}{4}\overset{\bullet}{} \\
4\,4.33 \\
+\,3\,43.43 \\
\hline
431.10
\end{array}
$$

9. $68.8 \times 14.7 \times 7.1 = 68.8 \times 104.37 = 7180.656$

10. $3.7 \times 8.2 \times 10.8 - 29.921 = 327.672 - 29.921 = 297.751$

11. $2.5 \times 1.5 = (2 + 0.5)(2 - 0.5) = 4 - (0.5)^2 = 4 - 0.25 = 3.75$

12.
$$\frac{15.75}{2.25} = 0.7 \times x$$
$$\Rightarrow \quad x = \frac{7}{0.7} = 10$$

13. $3.5 + 11.25 \times 4.5 - 32.5 = 3.5 + 50.625 - 32.5 = 54.125 - 32.5 = 21.625$

14. $\because$
$$
\begin{array}{r}
9.2\overset{\bullet}{1}4 \\
3.452 \\
+\ 2.191 \\
\hline
14.857 \\
\end{array}
$$

and
$$
\begin{array}{r}
15.593 \\
\overset{\bullet\quad\bullet}{-1\,4.8\,5\,7} \\
\hline
00.736 \\
\end{array}
$$

$\therefore \quad 15.593 - 9.214 - 3.452 - 2.191 = 0.736$

15.
$$
\begin{array}{r}
\overset{\bullet\ \ \bullet\ \ \bullet}{6\,6\,6.6\,6} \\
\overset{\bullet\ \ \ \bullet}{0\,6\,6.6\,6} \\
0\,0\,6.6\,6 \\
0\,0\,6.0\,0 \\
+\ 0\,0\,0.6\,6 \\
\hline
7\,46.6\,4 \\
\end{array}
$$

$\therefore \quad 666.66 + 66.66 + 666 + 6 + 0.66 = 746.64$

16.
$$
\begin{array}{r}
0.30 \\
3.00 \\
3.33 \\
3.30 \\
3.03 \\
+\ 3\,3\overset{\bullet}{3}.00 \\
\hline
345.96 \\
\end{array}
$$

17. $(34.12)^2 - \sqrt{7396} = 1164.1744 - 86 = 1078.1744$

18. $(21.35)^2 + (12.25)^2 = 455.8225 + 150.0625 = 605.885$

19.
$$
\begin{array}{r}
3\,3\overset{\bullet\ \ \bullet}{4.41} \\
47.26 \\
1.25 \\
5.00 \\
0.66 \\
\hline
388.58 \\
\end{array}
$$

$\therefore \quad 334.41 + 47.26 + 1.25 + 5 + 0.66 = 388.58$

20. $\sqrt[3]{\sqrt{0.000064}} = \sqrt[3]{0.008} = 0.2$

9 : Factorization

Exercise 2

1. $\because$ $\hspace{6em} 4:6 = 2:3$

and $\hspace{6em} 6:9 = 2:3$

$\therefore$ First factor is $(2x - 3)$

and $\hspace{3em}$ second factor $= \dfrac{4}{2}x + \dfrac{9}{3} = (2x - 3)$

$\therefore \hspace{4em} 4x^2 - 12x + 9 = (2x - 3)(2x - 3)$

2. $\because$ $\hspace{6em} 6:9 = 2:3$

$\hspace{8em} 8:12 = 2:3$

$\therefore$ First factor is $(2x + 3)$

and second factor is $\left(\dfrac{6x}{2} - \dfrac{12}{3}\right)$ *ie,* $(3x - 4)$

$\therefore \hspace{4em} 6x^2 + x - 12 = (2x + 3)(3x - 4)$

3. $\because$ $\hspace{5em} 4:(-25) = 4:(-25)$

and $\hspace{4em} 16:(-100) = 4:(-25)$

$\therefore$ First factor is $(4x - 25)$

and second factor is $\left(\dfrac{4x}{4} - \dfrac{100}{(-25)}\right)$ *ie,* $(x + 4)$

$\therefore \hspace{4em} 4x^2 - 9x - 100 = (4x - 25)(x + 4)$

4. $x^2 - x + 2 = \left(x - \dfrac{1 + \sqrt{-7}}{2}\right)\left(x + \dfrac{1 - \sqrt{-7}}{2}\right)$

5. $\because$ $\hspace{6em} 1:11 = 1:11$

and $\hspace{6em} 7:77 = 1:11$

$\therefore$ First factor is $(x - 11)$

and second factor is $\left(\dfrac{1}{1}x - \dfrac{77}{11}\right)$ *ie,* $(x - 7)$

Hence, $\hspace{3em} x^2 - 18x + 77 = (x - 11)(x - 7).$

6. $\because$ $\hspace{6em} 15:21 = 5:7$

$\hspace{6em} (-20):(-28) = 5:7$

$\therefore$ First factor is $(5x + 7y)$

and second factor is $\left(\dfrac{15x}{5} - \dfrac{28y}{7}\right)$ *ie,* $(3x - 4y)$

$\therefore \hspace{3em} 15x^2 - xy - 28y^2 = (5x + 7y)(3x - 4y)$

7. $\therefore$ $\hspace{6em} 4:-12 = 1:-3$

and $\hspace{6em} 1:-3 = 1:-3$

$\therefore$ First factor is $(y - 3x)$

and second factor is $\left(\dfrac{4}{1}y - \dfrac{3}{(-3)}x\right)$ *ie,* $(4y + x)$

$\therefore \hspace{3em} 4y^2 - 11xy - 3x^2 = (y - 3x)(4y + x)$

8. By inspection $(a + 2)$ is a factor of given polynomial and let first and last term of quadratic polynomial are 1 and 4.

Now, coefficient of middle term $= \dfrac{1 + 1 + 2 + 8}{1 + 2} - (1 + 4) = \dfrac{12}{3} - 5 = -1$

$\therefore \qquad a^3 + a^2 + 2a + 8 = (a + 2)(a^2 - a + 4)$

9. Since $(x + 1)$ is a factor of given polynomial (By inspection).

Let first and last term of quadratic polynomial are 2 and 21.

$\therefore$ Coefficient of middle term $= \dfrac{2 + 19 + 38 + 21}{1 + 1} - (2 + 21) = 40 - 23 = 17$

$\therefore \ 2x^3 + 19x^2 + 38x + 21 = (x + 1)(2x^2 + 17x + 21) = (x + 1)(2x + 3)(x + 7)$

10. Let $x^2 + 2x = t$

$\therefore \qquad t^2 - 3t - yt + 3y = t(t - 3) - y(t - 3) = (t - 3)(t - y)$

$\qquad\qquad\qquad = (x^2 + 2x - 3)(x^2 + 2x - y)$

10 : Highest Common Factor (HCF)

Exercise 2

1. Let $\qquad\qquad P(x) = x^3 - 1$

and $\qquad\qquad Q(x) = x^4 + x^2 + 1$

$\qquad P(x) + Q(x) = x^3 - 1 + x^4 + x^2 + 1$

$\qquad\qquad\qquad = x^4 + x^3 + x^2$

$\therefore \qquad\qquad$ HCF $= x^2 + x + 1$

2. Let $\qquad\qquad P(x) = 2x^4 + 243x = 4x^4 + 486x$

and $\qquad\qquad Q(x) = 24x^3 - 54x = 216x^3 - 486x$

$\qquad P(x) + Q(x) = 4x^4 + 486x + 216x^3 - 486x$

$\qquad\qquad\qquad = 4x^4 + 216x^3 = 4x^3(x + 54)$

$\therefore \qquad$ Required HCF $= x + 54$

3. Let $\qquad\qquad P(x) = x^4 + 3x^2 - 4$

and $\qquad\qquad Q(x) = x^4 - 4x^2 + 3$

$\therefore \qquad P(x) - Q(x) = x^4 + 3x^2 - 4 - x^4 + 4x^2 - 3$

$\qquad\qquad\qquad = 7x^2 - 7 = 7(x^2 - 1)$

$\therefore \qquad$ Required HCF $= x^2 - 1$

4. Let $\qquad\qquad P(x) = 2(a^2 - b^2) = 6(a^3 - ab^2)$

and $\qquad\qquad Q(x) = 3(a^3 - b^3) = 6(a^3 - b^3)$

$\therefore \qquad P(x) - Q(x) = 6b^3 - 6ab^2 = -6b^2(a - b)$

$\therefore \qquad$ Required HCF $= a - b$

5. Let $\qquad\qquad P(x) = p^2 - p - 6 = (p - 6)(p + 1)$

and $\qquad\qquad Q(x) = p^2 - 3p - 18 = (p + 3)(p - 6)$

$\therefore \qquad$ Required HCF $= (p - 6)$

11 : Simple Equations

Exercise 2

1.
$$25x - 19 - 3 + 4x - 5 = 3x - 6x + 5$$
$\Rightarrow \qquad 29x - 27 = -3x + 5$
$\Rightarrow \qquad 32x = 32$
$\Rightarrow \qquad x = 1$

2.
$$\frac{9x + 18 - 11x + 8 + 8x}{24} = \frac{18x + x + 7}{24}$$
$\Rightarrow \qquad 6x + 26 = 19x + 7$
$\Rightarrow \qquad 13x = 19 \Rightarrow x = \dfrac{19}{13}$

3. $\because \qquad 7 \times 9 = 63 = 3 \times 21$
$\therefore \qquad x = 0$

4.
$$10 - 12x = 3x - 1$$
$\Rightarrow \qquad 15x = 11 \Rightarrow x = \dfrac{11}{15}$

5.
$$x - 7 + x - 9 + x - 6 + x - 10 = 0$$
$\Rightarrow \qquad 4x - 32 = 0$
$\Rightarrow \qquad x = 8$

6.
$$2x - 1 + 3x - 1 = 0$$
$\Rightarrow \qquad 5x = 2 \Rightarrow x = \dfrac{2}{5}$

7. $\because \qquad -6 \times 7 \neq 3 \times (-11)$
$\therefore \qquad x = \dfrac{-33 + 42}{-6 + 7 - 3 + 11} = \dfrac{9}{9} = 1$

8.
$$x + 2 + x + 1 = 0$$
$$x = \frac{-3}{2}$$

12 : Quadratic Equations

Exercise 2

1. $\dfrac{d}{dx}(6x^2 + 11x + 3) = \sqrt{121 - 72}$
$\Rightarrow \qquad 12x + 11 = \pm 7$
$\therefore \qquad 12x = -11 + 7$
and $\qquad 12x + 11 = -7$
$\Rightarrow \qquad x = \dfrac{-4}{12} = \dfrac{-1}{3}$
and $\qquad x = \dfrac{-18}{12} = \dfrac{-3}{2}$

2. $\dfrac{d}{dx}(48x^2 - 13x - 1) = \sqrt{169 + 192}$

$\Rightarrow \qquad\qquad\qquad\qquad 96x - 13 = \pm 19$

$\Rightarrow \qquad\qquad\qquad\qquad 96x - 13 = 19,$

$\qquad\qquad\qquad\qquad\qquad 96x - 13 = -19$

$\Rightarrow \qquad\qquad\qquad\qquad\quad x = \dfrac{1}{3},$

$\qquad\qquad\qquad\qquad\qquad\quad x = \dfrac{-1}{16}$

3. $(x + 4) + \dfrac{1}{x + 4} = 9\dfrac{1}{9}$

$\Rightarrow \qquad\qquad x + 4 = 9 \ \text{ or } \ x + 4 = \dfrac{1}{9}$

$\Rightarrow \qquad\qquad\quad x = 5 \ \text{ or } \qquad x = -\dfrac{35}{9}$

4. $\dfrac{x}{x + 4} + \dfrac{x + 4}{x} = 12\dfrac{1}{12}$

$\Rightarrow \qquad\qquad \dfrac{x}{x + 4} = 12 \qquad \text{or} \qquad \dfrac{x}{x + 4} = \dfrac{1}{12}$

$\Rightarrow \qquad\qquad x = 12x + 48 \qquad \text{or} \qquad 12x = x + 4$

$\Rightarrow \qquad\qquad x = -\dfrac{48}{11} \qquad\quad \text{or} \qquad x = \dfrac{4}{11}$

5. $\therefore N_1 + N_2 = 19x + 7 + 6x - 39$

$\qquad\qquad\qquad\qquad\qquad = 25x - 32$

and $\qquad\qquad D_1 + D_2 = 12x - 11 + 13x - 21$

$\qquad\qquad\qquad\qquad\qquad = 25x - 32$

$\Rightarrow \qquad\qquad N_1 + N_2 = 0$

$\Rightarrow \qquad\qquad 25x - 32 = 0$

$\Rightarrow \qquad\qquad\qquad x = \dfrac{32}{25}$

and $\qquad\qquad N_1 - D_1 = 0$

$\Rightarrow \qquad\qquad 19x + 7 - 12x + 11 = 0$

$\Rightarrow \qquad\qquad\qquad x = -\dfrac{18}{7}$

15 : Simultaneous Equations

Exercise 2

1. Here, $a_1 = 1, b_1 = -1, c_1 = 3, a_2 = 3, b_2 = -2, c_2 = 10$

$\therefore \qquad x = \dfrac{(-1)(10) - (-2)(3)}{3 \times (-1) - 1 \times (-2)} = \dfrac{-10 + 6}{-3 + 2} = \dfrac{-4}{-1} = 4$

and $\qquad y = \dfrac{3 \times 3 - 1 \times 10}{3 \times (-1) - 1 \times (-2)} = \dfrac{9 - 10}{-3 + 2} = \dfrac{-1}{-1} = 1$

2. Here, $a_1 = 2, b_1 = -5, c_1 = -8, a_2 = 1, b_2 = -4, c_2 = -7$

$\therefore \qquad x = \dfrac{(-5)(-7) - (-4)(-8)}{1 \times (-5) - 2 \times (-4)} = \dfrac{35 - 32}{-5 + 8} = \dfrac{3}{3} = 1$

and $\qquad y = \dfrac{2 + 8}{5} = 2$

3. $\because \qquad x + y = 1$ ...(i)

and $\qquad x - y = 3$ ...(ii)

From Eqs. (i) and (ii), we get

$$x = 2, \, y = -1$$

4. $\because \qquad x + y = 2$ ...(i)

and $\qquad x - y = 4$ ...(ii)

From Eqs. (i) and (ii)

$$x = 3, \, y = -1$$

5. $\because 3 : 9 :: 17 : 51 :: 1 : 3$

$\therefore \qquad x = 0, \, y = \dfrac{51}{9} = \dfrac{17}{3}$

17 : Partial Fractions

Exercise 2

1. Let $\qquad \dfrac{2x + 3}{(x + 1)(x - 3)} = \dfrac{A}{x + 1} + \dfrac{B}{x - 3}$

$\therefore \qquad A = \dfrac{2(-1) + 3}{(-1 - 3)} = \dfrac{1}{-4}$

and $\qquad B = \dfrac{2 \times 3 + 3}{3 + 1} = \dfrac{9}{4}$

Hence, $\qquad \dfrac{2x + 3}{(x + 1)(x - 3)} = \dfrac{9}{4(x - 3)} - \dfrac{1}{4(x + 1)}$

2. Let $\dfrac{16}{(x - 2)(x + 2)^2} = \dfrac{A}{x - 2} + \dfrac{B}{x + 2} + \dfrac{C}{(x + 2)^2}$

$\therefore \qquad A = \dfrac{16}{(4)^2} = \dfrac{16}{16} = 1$

$\qquad C = \dfrac{16}{-2 - 2} = \dfrac{16}{-4} = -4$

and $\qquad B = \dfrac{d}{dx}\left(\dfrac{16}{x - 2}\right)_{\text{at } x = -2} = \left[\dfrac{-16}{(x - 2)^2}\right]_{\text{at } x = -2} = -1$

$\therefore \qquad \dfrac{16}{(x - 2)(x + 2)^2} = \dfrac{1}{x - 2} - \dfrac{1}{x + 2} - \dfrac{4}{(x + 2)^2}$

3. $\because \dfrac{x^3 - 2x^2 - 13x - 12}{x^2 - 3x - 10} = x + 1 - \dfrac{2}{x^2 - 3x - 10}$

Now, $\qquad \dfrac{2}{x^2 - 3x - 10} = \dfrac{A}{x - 5} + \dfrac{B}{x + 2}$

$\therefore$ $$A = \frac{2}{5+2} = \frac{2}{7}$$

and $$B = \frac{2}{-5-2} = -\frac{2}{7}$$

$\therefore$ $$\frac{x^3 - 2x^2 - 13x - 12}{x^2 - 3x - 10} = (x+1) - \frac{2}{7}\left(\frac{1}{x-5}\right) + \frac{2}{7}\left(\frac{1}{x+2}\right)$$

5. $\dfrac{x^2 + x + 1}{(x-1)^4}$

Let $x - 1 = y$ $\Rightarrow$ $x = y + 1$

$\therefore$ $$\frac{x^2 + x + 1}{(x-1)^4} = \frac{y^2 + 3y + 3}{y^4} = \frac{1}{y^2} + \frac{3}{y^3} + \frac{3}{y^4}$$

$$= \frac{1}{(x-1)^2} + \frac{3}{(x-1)^3} + \frac{3}{(x-1)^4}$$